D0947892

SOLID GROUND CHRISTIAN BOOKS

"Jesus Tempted in the Wilderness is Adolphe Monod at his best. It is a masterpiece, bringing together profound comfort, realistic understanding, practical wisdom, and heavenly glory for every believer and, in a special way, for those who are preparing for or are working directly in some ministry. By the Spirit's grace, if you digest Monod's book slowly, seriously, and prayerfully, you will make great spiritual gain as you engage in holy warfare against your own temptations and lusts. You really must read this book."

—JOEL R. BEEKE
President, Puritan Reformed Theological Seminary

"Here, in this spiritual gem, the greatest French preacher of the nineteenth century, Adolphe Monod, probes the implications of one of the most important of Christianity's mysteries: the terrible reality of the sinless Jesus being tempted in every area of human sin or vice. Firmly rooted in biblical orthodoxy, these three meditations reveal why Jesus was so tempted, how he emerged victorious, and what his victory means for us (pro nobis). Originally given to theological students at the old Calvinist seminary of Montauban in the traditional heartland of French Calvinism, these meditations are spiritual food and drink to all seeking to make progress in the Christian life. May God bless them to be such indeed!"

—MICHAEL A.G. HAYKIN
Professor, The Southern Baptist Theological Seminary;
Research Professor, Irish Baptist College

"No thoughts could penetrate so powerfully as these words about Jesus' temptations and ours. Just when you thought Monod could go no deeper, he takes you into the most inner recesses of the soul, adding comfort and hope to his searing realism about our weaknesses. In Constance Walker's translation, the author's voice is heard clearly again, bringing these messages to us in a life-transforming way."

—WILLIAM EDGAR
Professor, Westminster Theological Seminary

"Monod shows that Christ is our Savior because as 'the second Adam' He fulfilled in the desert what the first Adam failed to do in a garden. This book faithfully shows that in Christ we too can have victory over Satan and that it is God's word that is our weapon against the enemy of our souls."

—PAUL D. KOOISTRA
Coordinator, Mission to the World (Presbyterian Church in America)
Former President, Covenant Theological Seminary

"I read the meditations on temptation, and my heart was strangely touched. Two significant thoughts came to mind: 1) I never heard anything like that when I was in training for ministry, and 2) I am not sure my students are hearing anything like that today. The first, I cannot change, though perhaps it is not yet too late that I have heard these words of encouragement; the second I can correct. There are important warnings and encouragements that every seminary student needs to hear."

—R.J. GORE
Professor, Erskine Theological Seminary
Chaplain (COL), U. S. Army Reserve

"I first encountered Adolphe Monod's, *Jesus Tempted in the Wilderness* as I was battling intense discouragement. Because I was preparing for full-time Christian ministry overseas, I was reluctant and almost embarrassed to admit my struggle, yet Monod's book spoke to the heart of my inner turmoil with all the eloquence of a Christian classic. Monod showed me that all followers of Christ will, like their Master, face temptation, especially during seasons of preparation for ministry. Yet we too can have the hope of victory and can look to Christ to show us 'the means through which we can triumph.' Ultimately, God used my season of discouragement to build up and strengthen my faith, just as Monod had assured me He would. Monod's careful analysis of Christ's temptation points us to a vibrant faith that can not only survive, but actually thrive amidst the trials and travails that God allows to be placed in our path."

—A RECENT COLLEGE GRADUATE

JESUS

Tempted IN

THE WILDERNESS

Other Titles by Adolphe Monod

Living in the Hope of Glory

"Monod's dying testimony is instructing, enriching, inspiring."
—RICK PHILLIPS

An Unidivded Love: Loving and Living for Christ

"With unequaled passion and clarity he brings the unassuming listener not merely to the foot of the cross, but to Jesus himself."
—WILLIAM EDGAR

Woman: Her Mission and Her Life

"No woman can thoughtfully read this small volume without being influenced for the better."
—REV. W.G. BARRETT

Forthcoming Title

Saint Paul

(Five Discourses on Paul's impact and on his example to help reignite the Church to transform the world today.)

JESUS

Tempted IN

THE WILDERNESS

SHARING CHRIST'S VICTORY

ADOLPHE MONOD

CONSTANCE K. WALKER
EDITOR AND TRANSLATOR

SOLID GROUND
CHRISTIAN BOOKs
P.O. BOX 660132 • VESTAVIA HILLS • ALABAMA 35266

Unless otherwise indicated, all Scripture quotations are taken from The Holy Bible, English Standard Version, copyright © 2001 by Crossway Bibles, a division of Good News Publishers. Used by permission. All rights reserved.

Scripture quotations marked KJV are taken from the Authorized (King James) Version of the Holy Bible.

Cover image courtesy of Ken Jenkins
[For other examples of his work, please visit www.kenjenkins.com.]

Cover design by Borgo Design

Printed in the United States of America

978-159925-246-9

Contents

Adolphe Monod, 1802-1856

Biographical Sketch

Adolphe Monod (1802-1856) has rightly been called "The Voice of the Awakening." Those who came out of curiosity to hear the preaching of a celebrated orator would often leave the service pierced to the heart by his message, while the mature Christians in his congregations came back again and again to be transported by his preaching into the very presence of God and to have their faith stretched and challenged. Others, including Aldophe's older brother, Frédéric, were more influential as leaders of the movement that swept across France and Switzerland in the early 19th century, but none could expound the central core of its faith quite as clearly or persuasively or appealingly as Adolphe Monod.

Yet Monod's faith did not come without a struggle. He was descended from protestant ministers and received a clear call to the ministry at age fourteen, but the faith he grew up with was more formal than vibrant. In 1820 he entered seminary in Geneva, where the varied theological viewpoints soon left him in a state of spiritual confusion. He was often drawn toward the teaching of the Awakening, especially as presented by a Scotsman, Thomas Erskine, but his reason could not accept all of its teachings. Still confused, he accepted ordination in 1824.

Confusion turned to crisis when he agreed to pastor a group of French-speaking protestants in Naples. He knew he could not express his doubts to the congregation, but his natural candor recoiled at preaching something he did not yet believe. Family members prayed earnestly for him, and once again he received help through a visit by Thomas Erskine. Eventually, on July 21, 1827, he reached a state of peace. "I wanted to make my own religion, instead of taking it from God. . . . I was without God and burdened with my own well being, while now I have a God who carries the burden for me. That is enough." He still had questions, but he knew he would find the answers in the pages of the Bible.

Shortly thereafter he was called to join the pastoral staff of the large but worldly Reformed Church in Lyon, where his bold, gospel-centered preaching soon drew opposition. He was told not to preach salvation by grace; he refused. They demanded his resignation; he refused. After much unpleasantness, the leaders secured the government's permission to dismiss him, but a group of evangelical Christians who had already left the national church asked him to establish an independent congregation in Lyon. He served there until an unexpected call led him to the national church's seminary in Montauban. A decade later, in 1847, he returned to the pastorate, serving the Reformed Church in Paris. Quite ill and diagnosed with terminal cancer in 1855, he began holding small communion services in his home. These continued until his death on April 6, 1856, with his children writing down the brief meditations he gave.

Those facts, however, fail to truly capture the spirit of the man. His was a strong and passionate faith, in part because of his early spiritual struggles. He was also a man of great integrity, a keen mind, and a deeply caring, pastoral heart. All of these qualities were augmented and set off by his natural gift for speaking. Yet even as his renown grew, Adolphe Monod remained a truly humble man. A week before his death he said, "I have a Savior! He has freely saved me through his shed blood, and I want it to be known that I lean uniquely on that poured out blood. All my righteous acts, all my works which have been praised, all my preaching that has been appreciated and sought after—all that is in my eyes only filthy rags."

TRANSLATOR'S PREFACE

Adolphe Monod's seminary years and the years immediately following them were times of great spiritual struggle.
Perhaps this helps explain his special fondness and burden
for young men preparing for gospel ministry. Later, as a
seminary professor, he invited students to his home for tea.
This was unusual enough at Montauban to bewilder them at
first, but the visits ultimately produced strong and enduring
bonds of friendship between teacher and pupils.

During those years in academia, Adolphe Monod gave
three messages on temptation in the seminary chapel. As was
often his custom, he took his lessons primarily from the
earthly life of his Savior, in this case from Jesus tempted in
the wilderness. Material uniquely applicable to the seminary
students was removed when the messages were preached in
the Paris pulpit but was reinstated when they were published.
It is that published form[1] that is presented here in a new
translation. As in my earlier translations of Monod's works,[2] I
have attempted to retain his gracious romantic style while still
making the text flow naturally to a modern reader.

We will all be tempted at some point—no, at many
points—and the temptations are often most severe as we
begin a new work for the Lord. This was Monod's conviction
as he addressed his mid-19th-century students, and it is the

---

[1] The French text used here was from *Sermons, Deuxième Édition, Deuxième
Série*, Paris, Librarie de Ch. Meyrueis et Comp., 1857.

[2] *Living in the Hope of Glory* (Phillipsburg NJ, P&R Publishing, 2002) is a
new edition of Monod's *Farewells*, a series of short meditations given on
his death bed; *An Undivided Love* (Vestavia Hills AL, Solid Ground Christian Books, 2009) is a collection of seven of Monod's best sermons.

common experience of Christians today. Monod's burden was to warn us all, pastors and laity alike, to be on our guard. But expecting the attacks is not enough. He also wanted us to be wise in knowing how to counter them and confident of gaining a firm victory—the victory Jesus won for us. By carefully studying how Jesus faced the devil's temptations in the wilderness, every serious and fruitful Christian will be better equipped for his own spiritual battles.

Even as I worked on this book, I saw my husband live out its lessons, as he won his last battle of patient endurance with terminal cancer and went home to his Lord in glory.

Ken Jenkins' wild and majestic cover image, "Braids of Beauty," was chosen because it conveys the active drama of Jesus' battle with the enemy, the raw spiritual power engaged in the battle, and the joy of ultimate victory. C.S. Lewis uses a tall waterfall in his Narnia tales. In the creation story, *The Magician's Nephew*, the young hero must get above the waterfall at the border of Narnia to traverse the high, wooded Western Wild and reach an Eden-like garden where he is tempted by an evil witch. In *The Last Battle*, the victorious saints, now in glory, are able to swim up the heavenly waterfall, going "further up and further in" into the new Narnia.

I want to thank Sarah G. Byrd and Suzanne E. Schenkel for reading and correcting this edition of *Jesus Tempted in the Wilderness*. I am also deeply grateful to Michael Gaydosh and Solid Ground Christian Books for their sincere appreciation of Adolphe Monod's spiritual wisdom, for their shared vision of the importance of this monograph, and for their confidence in my ability, under God's guidance, to faithfully make these messages come alive again for 21st century readers.

May God use these simple discourses to bring great blessing, peace, strength, and victory into your lives.

Constance K. Walker
Durham, North Carolina

DEDICATION ෴

TO MY FORMER STUDENTS

My dear friends,

The meditations I publish today, after delivering them in Paris, were first given in Montauban at the beginning of a series of discourses on *The Example of Jesus Christ*. When I was speaking in the seminary chapel before you and, above all, *for* you, I sowed these discourses with allusions to your future career. I had to remove them when speaking from the pulpit in Paris, but I am reinstating them for publication. My heart is so eager to renew my interactions with you—interactions which have been too much interrupted by time, by space, and, sadly, by my illness—that I would seem to be lacking in faithfulness if I diverted these messages from their original purpose. Yet neither time nor space nor even my illness—nothing can chill the memory I have of you or loosen the bond that unites me to you in the Lord. Beyond that, to preach to the churches' leaders is to preach to the churches themselves, and the warnings given to the pastors are not foreign to any of the faithful, since none is without a ministry.

If those who read this small book become simpler in their faith, holier in their lives, more faithful in their service, then my joy will only be equaled by my gratitude toward the Author of every gift, especially—dare I say it?—if it is to you that he has done good through me.

Oh, my friends, for each of us the day is far gone; the night is at hand, so let us make haste! But for the church, "the night is far gone; the day is at hand" (Rom. 13:12), so let us awake!

Vester in nostro
A. M.

Paris, November 1853

SCRIPTURE TEXT Ș

And Jesus, full of the Holy Spirit, returned from the Jordan and was led [in]¹ the Spirit in the wilderness for forty days, being tempted by the devil. And he ate nothing during those days. And when they were ended, he was hungry. The devil said to him, "If you are the Son of God, command this stone to become bread." And Jesus answered him, "It is written, 'Man shall not live by bread alone.' "² And the devil took him up and showed him all the kingdoms of the world in a moment of time, and said to him, "To you I will give all this authority and their glory, for it has been delivered to me, and I give it to whom I will. If you, then, will worship me, it will all be yours." And Jesus answered him, "It is written,

> " 'You shall worship the Lord your God, and him only shall you serve.' "

---

¹ Literal translation. This expression, *in the Spirit*, does not correspond exactly to the one Matthew uses, *by the Spirit*. It ordinarily designates the special and miraculous way in which the Holy Spirit operates on those men whom he inspires, whether causing them to speak or to act. It is *in the Spirit* that Simeon comes to the temple (Luke 2:27). It is *in the Spirit* that Saint John receives the vision of the Apocalypse (Revelation 1:10); it is *in the Spirit* that he is carried away by an angel into the wilderness (Revelation 17:3), much as Ezekiel was lifted up and brought from one place to another through prophetic action (Ezekiel 8:3; 11:1). [A.M.]

² The Bible version that Monod was using, like the King James Version in English, adds the phrase, "but by every word of God," as in Matthew's account of the temptation.

And he took him to Jerusalem and set him on the pinnacle of the temple and said to him, "If you are the Son of God, throw yourself down from here, for it is written,

> " 'He will command his angels concerning you, to guard you,'

and

> " 'On their hands they will bear you up, lest you strike your foot against a stone.' "

And Jesus answered him, "It is said, 'You shall not put the Lord your God to the test.' " And when the devil had ended every temptation, he departed from him until an opportune time.

———————

[Read also Matthew 4:1-10 and Mark 1:12-13]

———————

first meditation

THE BATTLE

THE BATTLE

INTRODUCTION

My dear friends,

All of Scripture takes on a completely different aspect depending on whether it is seen through eyes of human wisdom or through eyes of faith, but nowhere is this difference more palpable than on the page we just read. I can recall a time when I could not meet this passage without a sense of embarrassment for my intellect and almost for the Word of God, whereas today I seek it as a favorite place, where my soul finds delightful and abundant food. It is as filled with healthy instruction for the little child who relates with simplicity to the witness of God, as it is filled with mysteries for the philosopher who pretends to judge the Scriptures instead of being judged by them.

THE MYSTERIES OF JESUS' TEMPTATION

There is mystery in the personal existence of the devil and in the insidious influence he exerts over us. This influence is so clearly attested to by the Scriptures that it cannot be denied without contradicting them.[1] But what is its origin, its nature, its scope? Of all this, we know nothing, or almost nothing. There is mystery in the ability granted to the devil to place unworthy snares before the very Son of God. That he should tempt us who are enslaved to his control through sin can be conceived, but how does one conceive of him being permitted to tempt the "Lord of lords" (Revelation 17:14), "the Holy One" (Mark 1:24, etc.), the one on whom he "has no claim" (John 14:30)?

There is mystery in the nature of the temptation to which Jesus is subjected. He "has been tempted," yet he was "without sin" (Hebrews 4:15). Those two facts are expressly affirmed in the Scriptures, but try to go one step further, and you will find yourself blocked on every side. How can one explain a battle against temptation without an inner attracttion? But how can we reconcile that inner attraction with an uncompromised holiness? If Jesus could not give in, where is the glory of his triumph? If he could give in, what becomes of his divine nature?

Finally, there is mystery in the way in which the scene of my text unfolds. Everything points to a true story as its basis: the tone of the narrative, the place of the event, the character of the book. Yet both the ensemble and the details of the text seem to show that it extends beyond the conditions of human experience. How can we remove this apparent contradiction? This is a struggle whose theater is the earth but whose actors are taken from heaven and hell; where does it take place? Is it in the visible world? Is it in the invisible world? Or could it be in some obscure border region that separates them and partakes of the nature of both.

Mystery upon mystery.

---

[1] Here the 19th century reader was referred to Adolphe Monod's sermon entitled *The Demoniacs*.

WHAT WE CAN KNOW

Without even trying to plumb the depths of these mysteries, I consider only the practical side of my text, which a child could grasp as well as we can and perhaps better. Guided by the Lord's words, "I have given you an example, that you also should do just as I have done" (John 13:15), let us seek in our text its instructions on how to conduct our lives.

In this terrible struggle between the Son of God and the spirit of darkness, we discern three main things: *the battle, the victory,* and *the weapons.* Each of the three is, in turn, going to instruct us. Through the battle that he endured, Jesus will teach us that we must expect to endure a similar battle. Through the victory that he won, Jesus will teach us that we, too, can be victorious. And through the weapons that he used, Jesus will teach us the means through which we can triumph. This matter is so extensive that I sense the need to devote three discourses to it. Today we will limit ourselves to the battle that Jesus had to endure in the wilderness.

JESUS' BATTLE AND OURS

Jesus' battle speaks to a pressing need of our hearts by reconciling us with the battle that we, too, must endure. You children of God who have some experience in the Christian life, I have no fear of being contradicted by you in saying that the temptations with which it is sown astonish and threaten to horrify you. Once we have entered into the Lord's paths, it seems to us as if the devil should be kept at a distance and no longer be allowed to touch us. When we experience his attacks, a secret fear grips us, as if the Lord were withdrawing from us. Our trouble grows if the temptation is prolonged and multiplies, if it surfaces in moments of communion with the Lord or if it fails to serve any purpose of which we might be aware. In the end, we can be thrown into a state bordering on despair. Jesus' battle speaks to all of that.

THE MEASURE OF JESUS' TEMPTATION

Jesus is tempted, and the battle you are going through is one that he went through before you. What am I saying? Next to his battle, yours scarcely deserves to be mentioned. There is temptation and then there is temptation. One temptation does not equal another, nor does the same temptation have the same strength for everyone. Therefore, to appreciate the temptation, one must take into account not only what it is inherently, but also what it is for the one exposed to it.

THE EXTERNAL CONDITIONS

Is it a matter of measuring what the temptation is in itself? You will find none amongst all your temptations that could be compared with the one that afflicts Jesus in my text. Think about it, and try to put yourself in his place. Imagine yourself separated from human society, thrown alone into the depths of the wilderness, surrounded by wild animals, deprived of all nourishment, with the devil at your side setting out one snare after another, and all of this goes on for forty days and forty nights.[2] This situation, in which you dare not imagine yourself, was that of your Savior.

THE INTERNAL DISPOSITIONS

But let us probe deeper. The true measure of the temptation is not in its external conditions; it is in the internal dispositions of the one whom it visits. The cold, defiling touch of a snake on the rough skin of a shepherd is one

---

[2] It follows from the evangelist's account that the Lord was tempted for forty days, and after this time had elapsed, the devil makes one last effort against him, the only effort that is described for us in detail. [A.M.]

thing; the same touch on the delicate skin of a young child is something quite different. In the same way, the tempter's attacks on a sinner like you or me are one thing; the same attacks on "the Holy One" (Mark 1:24) are something quite different.

If it is a dreadful thing for us to find ourselves trading blows with the spirit of darkness, tell me, what must it have been for the Son of God? As for us, conceived and born in iniquity, we are quite rightly subjected to the "ruler of this world" (John 12:31, 14:30, 16:11). His approach, his assaults, the blows that he inflicts—these are all in the natural course of things. But for the "only Son," the "beloved Son" to be, in turn, exposed to all this, isn't that a dreadful reversal? Must not his whole divine nature have risen up against the wilderness struggle with unspeakable horror? Whatever the case, here he is, engaged in it. Children of God, here is this only and beloved Son fighting, like you, against the eternal enemy of God and of his people.

Imagine yourselves living in Judea eighteen centuries ago and informed that the promised Messiah was somewhere in the world. Where would you have looked for him? I don't know, but you would have looked for him anywhere but where he actually was. You would not have looked for him in the humble workshop of the carpenter; you would not have looked for him amongst those being baptized by John on the shore of the Jordan River; above all, you would not have looked for him in the wilderness wrestling with the demon. Yet in order to find him, that is where you would have had to look, and throughout forty days and forty nights you would have looked elsewhere in vain.

HUMANITY'S COMMON LOT

But if you had finally discovered him there, would not the sight of his temptation have explained to you the inexplicable mystery of your own? "Ah, now I understand. The battle before which I draw back and in which I was ready to give way is the lot of humanity, a lot so inevitable that it could not even be spared him once that humanity became joined to the divine nature. Henceforth, let temptation come, even in its bitterest, most humiliating form. Nothing can surprise or alarm me any more!"

Seek Jesus Christ in the wilderness, Jacob at the river Jabbok (Genesis 32:22-32), Moses at Massah and Meribah (Exodus 17:1-7), Daniel in the lions' den (Daniel 6), and Saint John in his exile (Revelation 1:9)! Seek Saint Chrysostom in his disfavor,[3] John Huss before the Council of Constance,[4] and Luther at the Diet of Worms![5]

THE NATURE OF JESUS' TEMPTATION

Jesus "has been tempted," but how? "In every respect" (Hebrews 4:15), replies the Holy Spirit. Yes, truly "in every respect." Follow him in the light of my text, and you will see him tempted at all times, in all places, and in all ways.

AT ALL TIMES

Jesus was tempted at all times. "All these are but the beginning of the birth pains" (Matthew 24:8) that later events will be careful to complete. "When the devil had ended every temptation," for the time being, "he departed from him," but

---

[3] Saint John Chrysostom was an Early Church Father and archbishop of Constantinople. He was ultimately deposed and banished, in large part because he denounced the misdeeds of those in high positions.

[44] John Huss was a Czech reformer influenced by the teachings of John Wycliffe. The Roman Catholic Church excommunicated him for heresy in 1411, and in 1415, the Council of Constance condemned him to be burned at the stake.

[5] Martin Luther was tried before the Diet of Worms in 1521 and was excommunicated from the Roman Catholic Church.

only "until an opportune time" (Luke 4:13). He will return to the attack—do not doubt it. He will return to it throughout the entire course of Jesus' career, but above all he will return to it when that career reaches its supreme and decisive moment. Having made a first bruising of the heel (Genesis 3:15) in the wilderness, he will make a second on Golgotha, so that Jesus, who began to tread on the serpent (Luke 10:19) in his solitude, might finish by bruising his head (Genesis 3:15) on the cross.

Thus the two most dreadful temptations come to be placed at the two extreme ends of the ministry of God's Son, opening and closing the series of temptations that successively assailed him over a span of three and a half years. The first is a temptation of desire, requiring that all the world's promises be rejected. The second is a temptation of suffering, requiring that all the rage of hell and even the anger of heaven be born.

This double temptation, that of the wilderness and that of the cross, will present itself on our path as well, and it will generally do so in the same order. At the beginning of the course of the Christian life, earthly desires need to be defeated through renouncement. Later, and above all in the last battle, the agony of the flesh and of the spirit needs to be mastered through patience. "If anyone would come after me, let him deny himself and take up his cross and follow me" (Matthew 16:24).

IN ALL PLACES

Jesus was tempted in all places. Here we have no need to leave our text. We find there that Jesus is tempted in the wilderness, tempted on the mountain, tempted in the holy city.

There are men who have withdrawn into the wilderness to remove themselves from temptation. What peculiar blindness! Have they thus forgotten that the wilderness is where the Lord was tempted? You can flee the society of your peers, but how will you flee from Satan and your own heart? In league together against you, that external enemy and that internal enemy will follow you wherever you go. You will encounter temptation everywhere: in the wilderness, on the mountain, in the holy city—that is to say, in solitude, in the world, in the church. It is not a matter of fleeing it but of fighting it. It is not a matter of exchanging the temptations of one situation for those of another (which will be all the more dangerous because you have chosen and sought them) but of holding firm against the temptations of the situation in which God has placed you.

In All Ways

Finally, and this is my main point, Jesus was tempted in all ways. Here again I call upon my text. The devil only stops after having "ended every temptation." Of all the temptations to which Jesus was subjected, that of the wilderness is the most complete and best characterized. We see every effort of the enemy focused there, exhausting in turn all the resources and methods he possesses.

It is more than a temptation; it is *the* temptation. It is a system, an extended course in temptation. For the demon has a plan that it is good for us to understand and that the Holy Spirit reveals to us: "the desires of the flesh and the desires of the eyes and pride" (1 John 2:16).[6] He followed this plan with Eve, who gave in to the temptation on seeing first "that the tree was good for food," then "that it was a delight to the

---

[6] The order in which the apostle names the three great human lusts could not have been selected at random, especially since the same order is found in the temptation of Eve as well as that of Jesus as it is set forth in Saint Luke. It seems that the three temptations are ordered here according to their degree of subtlety. The first is a temptation of the flesh; the second a temptation of the eyes; the third a temptation of the spirit. [A.M.]

eyes," and finally "that the tree was to be desired to make one wise" (Genesis 3:6). He equally follows it with Jesus, whom he tempts first through the needs of the flesh, then through the spectacle of worldly pomp, and finally through the pride associated with a striking wonder.

In all of this, the devil's intention will appear even more clearly if, instead of looking at the object of the temptation, you probe its spirit. Satan seeks to make the Lord fall, in the beginning through a spirit of defiance towards God, in the middle through a spirit of unfaithfulness to God, and at the end through a spirit of reckless confidence in God. He successively appeals to the lack of faith, the forgetting of faith, and the abuse of faith. How well all of that is calculated, put together, and carried out, right through to the end!

Beyond that, there is nothing that does not serve as an instrument for the tempter. Whatever might be lacking in his own resources he borrows from those that are used against him, making weapons for himself out of the very means of resistance. Jesus has just heard a voice declaring him to be the Son of God, and the devil seeks to seduce him through that title of glory. Jesus has been clothed by the Holy Spirit with superhuman virtue, and the devil seeks to make him abuse his power. Jesus fasts, and the devil seeks to push him to the limit through hunger. In order better to succeed, the traitor "disguises himself as an angel of light" (2 Corinthians 11:14). He plays the saint and resigns himself to use the holy things. The holy city, the holy temple, even the holy Word of God—everything is useful for his treacherous hands.

TEMPTED AS MESSIAH

Note in particular the use that the devil makes of the name Messiah, which Jesus bears. It is this very name that Satan takes as the fulcrum for his temptations. He is quite willing for Jesus to show himself as the Messiah, provided that it is not Messiah as he is described by the holy prophets but Messiah as the carnal Jews conceive of him. In this, he flatters himself that he will have better success if, in addressing Jesus, he addresses him as a Jew, and as a Jew interested in confirming the expectations of his fellow-citizens.

The Messiah possesses a power above that of man. Satan wants him to use it, not according to the prophets' understanding, in order to save men's souls, but according to the carnal Jews' understanding, in order to satisfy his desires and theirs: "If you are the Son of God, command this stone to become bread."

The Messiah is to inherit all the kingdoms of the world. Satan wants him to receive them, not according to the prophets' understanding, from the hand of the Father as the reward for his sacrifice, but according to the carnal Jews' understanding, without a battle and from the hand of the ruler of this world: "If you, then, will worship me, it will all be yours."

Finally, the Messiah has magnificent promises of protection and deliverance. Satan wants him to take advantage of them, not according to the prophets' understanding, in order to accomplish his work of mercy in spite of all obstacles and in spite of Satan himself, but according to the carnal Jews' understanding, in order to further his own glory and that of his people: "If you are the Son of God, throw yourself down from here."

The fallen spirit has so many twists, the serpent has so many coils, and it is so true that he spared nothing in order to make Jesus fall, if he were able to fall!

STOP COMPLAINING

Oh you, then, who are beset and almost overcome by temptations, stop complaining. When everything is conspiring together against you; when your efforts, your precautions, your supports, even your prayers turn into a snare for you; when you sense yourself to be without comfort, without strength, abandoned by men, separated from God, and ready to give back your anguished soul, then cast a glance, one single glance toward Jesus in the wilderness. Believe me, one moment spent with him during those forty cruel days would have left you with memories forever able to guard you against the doubts that an excess of temptation suggests to you and against the murmurings that it drags forth from you. If you make up for this missing moment of sight through your faith, your battered courage will be lifted up.

Is anything happening to you that did not happen to Jesus? Is anything happening to you that isn't well below what happened to him? No, no, children of God, your Father has not forgotten you. He is treating you as he treated his only and beloved Son. It is now that you are being "conformed to the image of his Son, in order that he might be the firstborn among many brothers" (Romans 8:29). "For we do not have a high priest who is unable to sympathize with our weaknesses, but one who in every respect has been tempted as we are, yet without sin. Let us then with confidence draw near to the throne of grace, that we may receive mercy and find grace to help in time of need" (Hebrews 4:15-16).

THE TIMING OF JESUS' TEMPTATION

Jesus is tempted, but when? After what and before what?

AFTER HIS BAPTISM

It is after his baptism, after his fervent prayer, after the heavens opened over his head, after the Holy Spirit descended on him, after the voice from heaven saying, "This is my beloved Son, with whom I am well pleased" (Matthew

3:17)—it is after all this and, according to Mark, even "immediately" after (Mark 1:12) that Jesus is tempted. It is this moment of glory and spiritual blessing that is chosen for the temptation. It is chosen by Satan, because that is when the Son of God arouses the fullest measure of his anger and jealousy. Yet at the same time, it is chosen by God, because that is when the Son is best strengthened against all the assaults of the enemy. Take care, then, not to see yourselves as abandoned by God as a prey to temptation. Perhaps Satan is only gathering his forces against you because outstanding favors have singled you out to receive his blows, while also preparing you to ward them off.

We were saying that temptation is the lot of humanity; let us add that extraordinary temptations are the privilege of the best among humanity. They are a test that God reserves for those heroes of the faith whom no obstacle can stop and whom no difficulty can astound. He reserves it for a Moses, a Samuel, a Jeremiah, a poor Canaanite woman, a centurion from Capernaum, a Saint Peter, a Saint Paul.

That's not all. The test of extraordinary temptations is not just reserved for the strongest, but also for their times of greatest strength. God spared them during that first period of their spiritual journey, when they were still only able to walk when sustained by the tender devotion of first love. It is like a touching law of Moses that exempted a newly married man from his military obligations for a year, so that "he shall be free to be at home . . . to be happy with his wife whom he has taken" (Deuteronomy 24:5). But after the strength based on feeling has given way to another, more practiced and less variable strength, the strength of faith that knows how to "believe against hope" (see Romans 4:18), that is when the times of fatigue and warfare come; that is when the Lord calls his children to the harder battles that maintain and develop their holy courage.

Suppose you have just been baptized with a new baptism of the Holy Spirit. You have just poured your whole heart out before God in a humble and fervent prayer. You have just seen heaven open in some measure above you. You have just heard the voice of God who bears witness with your Spirit that you are a child of God (Romans 8:16). Do you therefore believe yourself to be sheltered, for the moment at least, from the attacks of the evil one? Don't be deceived. This is precisely the moment to expect his attacks and to place a double guard around your heart. Therefore watch and pray. But this is also the moment for which God has taken care to strengthen you beforehand. Therefore take courage. It was when Saint Paul had been "caught up to the third heaven" (2 Corinthians 12:2), that he was given "a thorn . . . in the flesh, a messenger of Satan to harass" him (2 Corinthians 12:7).

BEFORE HIS TIME OF MINISTRY

And before what is Jesus tempted? He is tempted before, immediately before the start of his ministry. He is tempted on the eve of entering a career totally devoted to the glory of God, to the salvation of men, and to the most holy work that ever was. As long as Jesus dwells in Nazareth, hidden in communal life and in Joseph's workshop, we hear nothing about the devil going to seek him. But as soon as he enters public life and devotes himself to the mission he has received from his heavenly Father, there he is, stopped at the very first step. Therefore don't be surprised if you see temptation approaching and redoubling its force when you set your hand to some good work, to some godly foundation, to some enterprise approved by God and men.

You, above all, young servants of the Lord preparing yourselves for the ministry of the Word in his church, do not think that "something strange" is "happening to you" (1

Peter 4:12) if the time you spend in this holy preparation is a
period of singular trial for your soul.

As long as you lived, gently ignored, in the confines of
the family home, the faith that you imbibed from infancy and
that became second nature to you only grew with the years
and seemed to be so deeply rooted in you that no storm
could ever shake it. But today you are deprived of the vigilant
oversight of a father and the tender counsels of a faithful
mother. Today you are placed in the presence of an unbe-
lieving and profane world that tolerates everything except
what is holy and true. Today you have entered far enough
into the knowledge of the things of God to raise more than
one embarrassing question, yet not far enough to resolve
them. With fear, you sense thoughts of doubt slipping in and
insinuating themselves into your heart.

Do not be disturbed, my young friend. This is the common story of all those who have preceded you down this
road. It is the story of even the holiest and most faithful
among them. The "enemy has done this" (Matthew 13:28),
and has done it because he sees you so usefully occupied. He
would perhaps agree to leave you in greater peace if you
would agree to bury the talent you received from the Lord.
Then in causing you to fall, he would be hurting only you.
Now, however, it is your future ministry that he hopes to
hinder; it is all the people he hopes to deprive of the word of
life, if he robs you of "your most holy faith" (Jude 20). That
is what makes him so active and vigilant. The work of the
Holy Spirit and the work of the demon are closely linked.
The first provokes the second, and, in the invisible world,
heaven borders on hell. The Holy Spirit leads Jesus into the
wilderness, where he is tempted by the devil, and Satan, as he
was getting ready to tempt Job, appeared "in the heavenly
places" (Ephesians 6:12) among the "sons of God" (Job 1:6).

Warned as you are by the example of the Lord himself,
wait for the tempter with firm resolve. "Resist the devil, and

he will flee from you" (James 4:7). Is he making you cold toward reading the Bible? Then meditate on it more attentively. Is he discouraging you in prayer? Then pray with greater ardor and perseverance. Is he turning you away from the simplicity of the faith? Then apply yourself to grow in the spirit of a small child, even as you grow in the learning of a theologian. When the enemy sees you thus turning his attacks to your strengthening, he will end up growing weary and will leave you in peace rather than do you such great good. Whatever the case, he will be unable to try anything against you but what Jesus Christ's temptation should have helped you foresee.

Here even the doctors of the synagogue can instruct you. One of their apocryphal books, Ecclesiasticus, begins its second chapter with these words: "My son, if you wish to serve the Lord, prepare yourself for temptation."

THE REASON FOR JESUS' TEMPTATION

Finally, Jesus is tempted, but why? A complete answer to that question touches on those mysteries we did not want to probe. Still, Scripture lets us know that Jesus "had to be" tempted. The apostle expressly tells us, "He had to be made like his brothers in every respect, so that he might become a merciful and faithful high priest in the service of God, to make propitiation for the sins of the people. For because he himself has suffered when tempted, he is able to help those who are being tempted" (Hebrews 2:17-18).

No doubt the temptation was also necessary for other reasons: to vindicate, through Jesus Christ's victory, the condemnation of man, who was defeated in the same battle; to fill up the measure of Messiah's redemptive suffering; to begin pointing him out to earth, heaven, and hell as the "Son of God" who "appeared . . . to destroy the works of the devil" (1 John 3:8); perhaps—how do we know?— to finish revealing this identity to him, to make him "perfect" (Hebrews 2:10, 5:9) through trial, and to cause him to begin running his race, "conquering, and to conquer" (Revelation 6:2).

Whatever the case, he had to be tempted, and that is enough for me.

PART OF MESSIAH'S MISSION

The temptation was not an accident in Jesus' life or career. Rather, it was useful, even essential. It was part of the plan for our redemption. All the images used by the prophets to depict the coming Messiah were meant to foreshadow a battle between him and the spirit of darkness, a battle for which the story recounted in our text is but the prelude. Because he had come to found a kingdom, but to found it on the ruins of a usurped power, the Messiah, the true Joshua (Hebrews 4:8), could only establish his rule through conquest. He could only gather "the inheritance of the nations" (Psalm 111:6) by snatching it away from the "ruler of this world" (John 12:31, 14:30, 16:11).

The Jews themselves understood this, and it was an article of their theology that the Messiah had to be tempted by Satan from the very beginning of his career. Our text, in turn, also recognizes this character of necessity in the temptation. Everything here is anticipated, brought together, and willed by God. Jesus is led, or, according to Saint Mark (1:12), driven by the Spirit into the wilderness where he is tempted by the devil.[7] Saint Matthew expresses himself in even more definite terms: "Jesus was led up by the Spirit into the wilderness to be tempted by the devil" (Matthew 4:1). The devil tempts him and then, when he "has ended every temptation,

---

[7] The gospel writer's expression "driven" has a particular force to it that signifies *thrown* or *hurled*. [A.M.]

he departs from him" (see Luke 4:13), as if having played his role. He can only do to Jesus, in tempting him as in crucifying him, "whatever [God's] hand and [God's] plan had predestined to take place" (Acts 4:28).

FOR THE PERFECTING OF THE SAINTS

Let us learn from this, my dear friends, that, for us as well, the temptations of which we complain are useful, even essential for "the perfecting of the saints" (Ephesians 4:12 KJV) and to shape us for the work God has given us to do in the world. Saint James says that "God . . . tempts no one" (James 1:13), because he never pushes us to sin, but he can "lead us . . . into temptation" (Matthew 6:13, Luke 11:4), as he did with regard to his Son, "testing us to know what is in our heart" (see Deuteronomy 8:2). If we resist the temptation, we come out of it stronger and more faithful, purified as "gold . . . tested by fire" (1 Peter 1:7). If we give in, then, no doubt, we bear the pain of our frailty, but even then, if repentance lifts us up again, we have at least learned to understand our weakness and to seek our strength only in the Lord.

It is in this unending struggle; it is from victory to victory and, alas, through the lack of consistent victory; it is in the midst of alternate victories and defeats that the healthy training of our faith goes on and grows. The storm overturns and uproots the tree that is poorly anchored in the soil, but it stirs and shakes the tree that is firmly held there only to force it to thrust still deeper the thousand hidden arms with which it penetrates and grips the ground.

The apostle writes that "suffering produces endurance, and endurance produces character, and character produces hope" (Romans 5:3-4),[8] and what is said here about

---

[8] To really understand these deep words, one must know that . . . *hope* is

suffering—the type of temptation most often dealt with in God's Word—is nevertheless true of all the other types. That's why the apostle Saint James exhorts us in his own distinctively energetic but paradoxical language to "count it all joy . . . when we meet temptations of various kinds" (see James 1:2).[9] He calls "blessed" not the man who is never tempted, but the one who "endures temptation" (that is, who undergoes it without giving in, see James 1:12 KJV), for "when he has stood the test he will receive the crown of life, which God has promised to those who love him" (James 1:12).[10]

TO COMPLETE THE WORK OF THE HOLY SPIRIT

If Jesus needed his temptation, we equally need ours. Satan's work is essential to complete the work of the Holy Spirit, and nothing arrives at perfection in this base world unless the devil has first put his hand on it.

Job needed that cruel unfolding of the evil one's malice to enlighten his faith, to strengthen his heart, and to make his joy complete. Daniel needed those treacherous detractors

---

not a more or less uncertain waiting, but the firm assurance of those good things to come that we as yet possess only by faith (Rom 8:24-25). When we are afflicted, we are being trained in patience; when we have suffered with patience, we understand that our faith is *the real thing*, and when our faith has been thus tested, we have a firm and glorious trust in the grace of the Lord. [A.M.]

[9] We render as *temptations* the word that all of our versions except for the 1839 Lausanne version have rendered as *trials*. [The English Standard Version (ESV) also renders it as *trials*.] Our translation seems to us to be required by the apostle's overall ideas, and in particular by verses 12-14, where these same versions felt obliged to translate the same word by *temptation* and the corresponding verb by *to tempt*. [The ESV uses *trial* in verse 12 and *tempt* in verses 13 and 14.] [A.M.]

[10] The word *endured* and the phrase *stood the test* have an equivocal sense, but in the original both suppose that the test has been passed and the temptation has been defeated. [A.M.]

who had him thrown into the lions' den to show him the full power and faithfulness of his God during the peaceful night spent among the dreadful beasts.

Saint Paul needed that "thorn . . . in the flesh, a messenger of Satan to harass" him, in order to maintain his humility, to keep him "from being too elated by the surpassing greatness of the revelations" (2 Corinthians 12:7), and to suggest to him the words "When I am weak, then I am strong" (2 Corinthians 12:10), words which consoled him and will console the saints until the end of time. Saint Peter needed the high priest's court to show him his own weakness and, after the confession and pardon of his sin, to make him reappear in the eyes of the church more worthy than ever of the distinction the Lord had accorded him and preserved for him in spite of his fall.

Chrysostom needed his master's anger; Saint Augustine needed the perils of his youth; Luther needed the mortal battles of his soul; Calvin needed his frail health and implacable foes.

And you, my dear brother, Satan seems to have chosen you as the object of his most formidable attacks, and his pride appears totally engaged in your fall. You find yourself reduced to the last extremity and at the point of giving in; you join in those anguished cries of the Messiah in the psalms, "The flood sweeps over me. I am weary with my crying out; my throat is parched. My eyes grow dim with waiting for my God" (Psalm 69:2-3). Yet you needed that. Yes, you can be sure, you needed even that, you needed all of that to teach you to serve God, to confound the great adversary, and to "rejoice with joy that is inexpressible and filled with glory" (1 Peter 1:8).

You are God's child, his beloved child, his privileged child. Truly, if we were able to lift ourselves up above the flesh and to judge according to God's Word, we would be more inclined to envy you than to pity you. "Therefore, do not throw away your confidence, which has a great reward" (Hebrews 10:35), but rather resist, hold firm right to the end, give glory to God, and abound in thanksgiving.

IN PREPARATION FOR MINISTRY

Young servants of God, if temptation is necessary for all, it is doubly so for you. The battle that you are beginning to wage against the world's opposition and, above all, against the natural unbelief of your own hearts should not astound you. It is the narrow way through which you must pass to arrive at a more solid faith. It is through the anguish of temptation that you will learn, like your Savior, to some day sympathize with the weaknesses of others and to help those who are tempted.

Listen to what was said on this subject by a great master as regards the Christian life, one who struggled valiantly against the powers of the world and of hell. Luther, writing to a young theologian, pointed out to him from Psalm 119 three principal means through which the psalmist strengthens himself in the divine life: prayer, meditation on the Scriptures, and temptation. Here is how he expresses himself on the last of the three.

> Temptation is the touch stone that will make you not only know and understand, but also experience how upright the Word of God is, how true, how sweet, how amiable, how powerful, how consoling, how wise above all other wisdom. Good preachers are not made without temptation—only pure babblers who don't know what they are talking about or why. They are, as Saint Paul said to Timothy, "desiring to be teachers of the law, without understanding either what they are saying or the things about which they make confident assertions" (1 Timothy 1:7).

You also see David complain often in our psalm of all sorts of enemies, oppressors, and stubborn, rebellious spirits with whom he must bear because he carries the Word of God with him everywhere. You likewise will no sooner have begun bearing witness to the Word of God than the devil will set about to tempt you. This will make you a good doctor and will, through the trials that he raises up for you, instruct you to search and to love the Word of life. I myself am under great obligation to my papists who, through all Satan's ruckus, have so mistreated me and reduced me to such extremity and anguish that they have ended up making me into a passable theologian—a state I would never have arrived at without them. As for what they have, on the other hand, gained from me, I willingly give over to them the honors, victories, and triumphs, which is all that they really want.[11]

PRAYER

Lord Jesus, we do not want to complain about temptation. We have found you today in the wilderness, and we will not refuse to follow you there. We have cast our gaze on what you suffered in being tempted, and we have been moved to the very depths of our hearts by it. You suffered in order to become like us; shall we not agree to suffer in order to be made like you? Yet we distrust ourselves, Lord, and we say to you, just as you taught us, "Lead us not into temptation!" (Matthew 6:13). But if we need to be led there, we add with confidence, as you again have taught us,

---

[11] Monod does not give the source of this quote, so the English text has been obtained by translating the French given in the sermon text.

"Deliver us from the evil one" (Matthew 6:13, alternate reading).

It is enough for us to recall that in you we have "a merciful and faithful high priest" who, "because he himself has suffered when tempted, . . . is able to help those who are being tempted" (Hebrews 2:17-18). Oh, how sweet that thought is to us, Lord! It teaches us that whatever our temptations may be, you knew them before us, and you have already conquered them on our behalf! That is why, oh our compassionate Savior, we "pour out our hearts before you" (see Psalm 62:8) with holy liberty. Though we should be tormented as much as you yourself were (if that were possible), we will "with confidence draw near to the throne of grace, that we may receive mercy and find grace to help in time of need" (Hebrews 4:16). It is not us that our common enemy is after; it is you. Yes, it is you and you alone that he is attacking in us. Thus it is also for you to defend us! Triumph over him in us! And since you have been tempted as we are, make us victors like yourself! Amen.

THE VICTORY

THE VICTORY

JESUS' VICTORY, OUR GUARANTEE

My dear friends,

Jesus' battle has reconciled us with the one that we ourselves must undergo. Now his victory will guarantee to us that we, in turn, can be victorious.

THE DOUBT THAT PLAGUES US

The thing that makes us weak against temptation is our uncertainty over the outcome of the battle. Nothing would be impossible for us if we were assured of overcoming, but doubt, that bitter doubt, destroys our courage.

You are tempted by a spirit of apathy. You would like to become "fervent in spirit" and "constant in prayer" (Romans 12:11-12), but you doubt that you will be able to rise above your spiritual lethargy. Thus you continue, in spite of yourself, to drag yourself like a coward along the path on which God invites you to run.

You are tempted by a spirit of grumbling. Under the weight of a cruel and prolonged affliction, you would like to abound in thanksgiving, but you doubt that you will be able to withstand the suffering that bears down on you.

Thus your life continues to be consumed in sterile and ungrateful complaints.

You are tempted by a spirit of unbelief. You would like to rest on God's Word with unshakeable confidence. You understand that this is your peace, your strength, your sanctification, but you doubt that you will be able to uproot a slowness to believe that is supported by temperament, by education, by example, and by habit. Thus you continue to waver miserably between the truth of God and the objections of the natural heart.

You are tempted by a spirit of sensuality. While abstaining from the excesses that would dishonor your Christian profession, you "make . . . provision for the flesh, to gratify its desires" (Romans 13:14). You feel the weight of a humiliating yoke that you are longing to shake off, but you doubt that you will be able to carry out a life of renouncement and sacrifice. Thus you continue to give yourself over to a self-centered and frustrating well-being.

JESUS' TOTAL VICTORY

Oh, you who recognize yourselves in this sad picture, come and learn through the story of my text that you can conquer every temptation. Jesus was tempted just as you are, and whereas the first Adam yielded in Eden, this second Adam overcame every trial in the wilderness. His victory is complete. After forty days of unceasing attacks, after a last desperate assault, the adversary finally found himself compelled to lift the siege, ashamed and convinced of his own powerlessness. Jesus thus gained the right to say, "The ruler of this world . . . has no claim on me" (John 14:30).

Not one of "the flaming darts of the evil one" (Ephesians 6:16) found the tiniest point of entry with him. It is written, he "in every respect has been tempted as we are, yet without sin" (Hebrews 4:15). No sin before the temptation and what led up to it; no sin after the temptation and what came out of it. In him we have "a high priest, holy, innocent, unstained, separated from sinners" (Hebrews 7:26). Very well, if Jesus overcame like that, you can overcome as he did.

UNFATHOMABLE MYSTERIES

Here again, we must begin by setting aside the mysterious side of our subject, along with the questions—more curious than useful—to which it gives rise. The analogy between Jesus' temptation and ours is not perfect, for we are children of a corrupt race who harbor within our hearts a covetousness that Jesus never knew. Though he took upon himself the infirmities that sin introduced into our nature, let us never think that he in any way participated in its corrupt leanings!

We can distinguish three kinds of temptation: that of Jesus, that of Adam, and our own. Jesus was "without sin" (Hebrews 4:15) both before and after the testing. Adam was without sin before the testing, but not after. We are without sin neither before nor after the testing. As Saint James shows us in his epistle, "Each person is tempted when he is lured and enticed by his own desire. Then desire when it has conceived gives birth to sin" (James 1:14-15).

This gives rise to questions with regard to the moral nature of temptation and the degree of holiness we can attain in this life, questions which have more than once troubled the church but which we judge it to be neither necessary nor even possible to plumb to their depths. Rather, I limit myself here to the application that concerns us in our present condition, and I let our subject remain on the practical ground to which the apostle James led us in the words I just quoted. It is a matter of preventing desire from conceiving and giving birth to sin. You always can do it.

WE CAN BE VICTORIOUS

Just as Jesus overcame his temptation and just as Adam could have overcome his, so too there is not one among all the temptations you encounter on your path that you cannot overcome. Thus you who are tempted by a spirit of apathy can "have life and have it abundantly" (John 10:10). You who are tempted by a spirit of grumbling can "rejoice always" (1 Thessalonians 5:16), "proclaiming thanksgiving aloud" (Psalm 26:7). You who are tempted by a spirit of unbelief can "continue in the faith, stable" (Colossians 1:23), "steadfast, immoveable" (1 Corinthians 15:58). And you who are tempted by a spirit of sensuality can "discipline [your] body and keep it under control" (1 Corinthians 9:27) and "by the Spirit . . . put to death the deeds of the body" (Romans 8:13).

You can do it, because Jesus has already done what you have to do.

VICTORY IN HIS HUMAN NATURE

Perhaps you will say to me, "Jesus was the Son of God. His victory cannot prove ours." If that objection were well founded here, it would be equally so elsewhere. We would have to give up proposing Jesus as an example to men, and in vain would the Holy Spirit have said, "Christ has left you an example, so that you might follow in his steps" (see 1 Peter 2:21).

But this objection has a cause that explains many other errors, both of doctrine and of practice: we fail to appreciate the Lord's human nature, or we at least lose sight of it. His humanity is just as essential to keep in mind as his divinity.

TEMPTED AS THE SON OF MAN

Yes, Jesus was the Son of God, but he was also the Son of man. Since he was tempted in his human nature, it is also in his human nature that he overcame temptation. Here, we do not intend to ignore the Lord's divine nature in our text's narrative. We do not forget that immediately prior to the temptation, Jesus was declared to be the Son of God, was filled with the Holy Spirit, and was thus fortified against the battle that awaited him. I only want you to notice, my dear friends, that in the gospel writers' narrative, only the Son of man appears in Jesus during the battle itself, while the Son of God fades into the background.

Actually, I'm wrong. He is seen, but only in Satan's discourses. It is Satan who recalls this title for Jesus and uses it to tempt him, sometimes through doubt, sometimes through presumption, sometimes through ambition. But Jesus makes no use of it to defend himself.

If he had wanted to display his divine power here, he could have appealed to his Father, and he would at once have sent him more than twelve legions of angels, as he himself declared in the other temptation that marked the end of his career (Matthew 26:53). But what am I saying? He had no need of angels. He had only to speak a word, and Satan would be knocked down, just as the men sent by the Sanhedrin were knocked down in the garden of Gethsemane (John 18:3-6). Yet he does nothing of the sort. He confines himself to the sphere of human action.

FIGHTING AS THE SON OF MAN

He fights against Satan with man's weaknesses and with the means at man's disposal. As a man he endures hunger and allows Satan to approach him, to reach him, and to tempt him. As a man he sustains himself through confidence in God and triumphs through God's strength.[1] Above all, it is

---

[1] See Ephesians 6:10 and following, where Saint Paul seems to allude to Jesus' battle. [A.M.]

as a man that he quotes the Scriptures, written by men for men. Just as elsewhere we see Jesus strengthened by an angel in his anguish, even though he is the one whom "God's angels worship" (Hebrews 1:6), so here we see Jesus leaning on Moses, even though he is Moses' Lord and Master. Astonishing fact! Marvelous fact!

What need did Jesus have to leaf through the books of his servant, as we do, in order to find answers to the seductions of the evil one? Couldn't he draw them out of his own depths? Isn't this "the only begotten Son, which is in the bosom of the Father" (John 1:18 KJV), the one who "is in heaven" (John 3:13, KJV) and "who warns from heaven" (Hebrews 12:25)? Yes, but here he had to speak "in an earthly way" to serve as an example to those who are "of the earth" (John 3:31).

This is true to the point that, not content to call only on the Scriptures, Jesus chose within the Scriptures only those passages that apply to all believers indiscriminately. He cites not one of the numerous witnesses referring exclusively to the Messiah and guaranteeing him victory,[2] having resolved to draw only on the common treasure of the whole Church. The stranger this is, the more its purpose is evident. Against a human temptation, Jesus gains a human victory through human means, in order to let men know that they can be victorious just as he was victorious.

VICTORY FOR HUMANITY

There is more. Not only was Jesus victorious *in* humanity, but he was victorious *for* humanity. Waging the wilderness battle as the Savior and representative of man, it is in man's name and in his behalf that he gains a victory whose fruit will be gathered by whoever hopes in his name.

---

[2] Psalm 110, Isaiah 63, etc. [A.M.]

If he had not been victorious for us, how would he be able, through his victory, to set our minds at ease concerning the world's anguishes? "In the world you will have tribulation. But take heart, I have overcome the world" (John 16:33). He alone has been able to "bind the strong man" (see Matthew 12:29), but once the strong man is bound, Jesus will not enter alone into the "strong man's house and plunder his goods" (Matthew 12:29); we too will enter in after him. Satan is already defeated before he even attacks us, and all the more powerless against us when he finds within us the very one who defeated him in the wilderness.

In Jesus, we are so well assured of victory that Scripture presents it to us as having already been obtained. "You are strong, and the word of God abides in you, and you have overcome the evil one" (1 John 2:14). In Jesus, all has been accomplished. "We are more than conquerors through him who loved us" (Romans 8:37). There remains for us only to associate ourselves with his victory, and in order to associate ourselves with it, we need only believe in his name. "For everyone who has been born of God overcomes the world. And this is the victory that has overcome the world—our faith" (1 John 5:4).

No doubt our adversary is formidable, this "roaring lion" who "prowls around . . . seeking someone to devour" (1 Peter 5:8), but he has ventured his strength in vain against "the Lion of the tribe of Judah, the Root of David," who "has conquered" (Revelation 5:5). To him the spirit of prophesy speaks saying, "From the prey, my son, you have gone up. He stooped down; he crouched as a lion and as a lioness; who dares rouse him?" (Genesis 49:9). He alone is invincible, and he is the one fighting for us. "For thus the Lord said to me, 'As a lion or a young lion growls over his prey, and when a band of shepherds is called out against him is not terrified by their shouting or daunted at their noise, so the LORD of hosts will come down to fight on Mount Zion and on its hill' " (Isaiah 31:4). Fear not, "for he who is in you is greater than he who is in the world" (1 John 4:4).[3]

Let us therefore be assured that Jesus' victory guarantees ours and that in him we will find true help, because he himself has experienced and overcome temptation. This is the Holy Spirit's thought in two passages that we have already cited from the Epistle to the Hebrews. "For because he himself has suffered when tempted, he is able to help those who are being tempted" (Hebrews 2:18). And he "in every respect has been tempted as we are, yet without sin. Let us then with confidence draw near to the throne of grace, that we may receive mercy and find grace to help in time of need" (Hebrews 4:15-16).

OVERCOMING DOUBTS

I could stop here. This doctrine is well enough established, especially in the context of our narrative. But the soul that labors and is heavy laden (Matthew 11:28) does not give in so quickly. It needs fresh encouragement, which I have no intention of refusing.

Two things trouble the soul that is facing temptation: its own weakness and the strength of the temptation. If we turn our eyes onto ourselves, we find we are too weak to defend ourselves, even against the most ordinary temptation. If we consider the temptation, we find it strong enough to overwhelm us, even when we are at our strongest. But let us draw near again to Jesus tempted in the wilderness, and his victory will reassure us in this two-fold consideration.

---

[3] Compare this passage with 2 Kings 6:16: "Do not be afraid, for those who are with us are more than those who are with them;" and with 2 Chronicles 32:7: "Be strong and courageous. Do not be afraid or dismayed before the king of Assyria and all the horde that is with him, for there are more with us than with him." [A.M.]

THE SOURCE OF JESUS' STRENGTH

You are weak, my dear brother; so weak, so flagging, so destitute, so beaten down in body and spirit that you find yourself unable to surmount the least temptation. Truly you *would* be unable if you had to triumph in your own strength, but do you think that our Lord triumphed in the wilderness in his own strength? Perhaps you consider him a stranger to all your grief,[4] tranquil, imperturbable. But who portrayed him to you that way? It is your imagination, not the Scriptures.

The Scriptures present the Messiah to us as "a man of sorrows, and acquainted with grief" (Isaiah 53:3). True, they are silent as to the state of his spirit during the battle in the wilderness, and it is not our place to make up for their silence or to say to what extent his forty-day fast might have exhausted his strength or broken his courage. Yet elsewhere the Scriptures show him to us in a distress that you have never known. In Gethsemane, "being in an agony he prayed more earnestly; and his sweat became like great drops of blood falling down to the ground" (Luke 22:44). On the cross, he cried to his God, "My God, my God, why have you forsaken me?" (Matthew 27:46, Mark 15:34).

Where, then, does Jesus find strength? In God. The spirit of the whole temptation is to detach him from God. The goal is to get him first to meet his own needs without God's providence, then to receive the heritage of the nations without God's gift, and finally to display his divine glory without God's command. But Jesus holds fast to God. It is not in his own strength that he struggles and triumphs; it is in his Father's strength.

---

[4] The word here rendered as *grief* is often better translated as *languishing*. The former is used here because in the next paragraph Monod cites Isaiah 53:3, where the same French word is used and where the English Standard Version has *grief*.

A QUESTION OF FAITH

Be instructed by this, my dear friends. If you are not as strong as Jesus, your God is no less strong than his God, so let his rock be your rock, and his strength will be your strength. For Jesus, for Adam, for you, it is not a question of strength; it is a question of faith. Your own strength cannot deliver you if you do not believe, nor can your own weakness hurt you if you do believe. Your weakness will even help you if you know how to deal with it properly, and through the sense you have of it pushing you to seek God's strength, you will experience the truth of the phrase, "When I am weak, then I am strong" (2 Corinthians 12:10).

Strange paradox! Sublime truth! Instead of stopping at merely discussing it, believe it, live it. My dear brother, are you flagging, impoverished, and beaten down in body and spirit, unable to surmount the least temptation? Good. You are precisely in the desired state for being victorious. It is now, when you are deprived of the illusions of pride and absolutely despairing of yourself, that you are going to "be strong in the Lord and in the strength of his might," and that you will "put on the whole armor of God, that you may be able to stand against the schemes of the devil" (Ephesians 6:10-11).

Hold fast to God, as the branch holds fast to the vine. In him you will "find grace to help in time of need" (Hebrews 4:16). Note well the phrase *in time of need*. Strength is promised to you for your moment of need. You would like to get it ahead of time, so that by casting a self-satisfied glance at your spiritual supplies you could reassure yourself about future terrors. But this is not the Lord's way. He does not give today the things for tomorrow, but he will certainly give today the things for today, and tomorrow for tomorrow. The man with the withered hand and to whom Jesus said, "Stretch out your hand" (Matthew 12:13, Mark 3:5, Luke

6:10) would never have stretched it out if he had waited to receive the required strength for this movement ahead of time, but at the Lord's word he stretched it out, and there it is, healed. "If you believe, you will see the glory of God" (see John 11:40).

GOD MEASURES THE TEMPTATION

You say again that the temptation is strong, terrible, overwhelming. But was Jesus' temptation any less so? Compare it with that of Adam. Scripture itself even invites us to make this comparison, for it is not without design that it places one of these temptations at the beginning of the Old Testament and the other at the beginning of the New Testament. In this case as in all the others, it contrasts the "last Adam" with the "first . . . Adam" (1 Corinthians 15:45).

Adam is tempted in Eden, which means *abode of delights*; Jesus is tempted in the wilderness. Adam is tempted in the midst of an abundance of all things; Jesus is tempted in a state of need and hunger. Adam is tempted once and falls; Jesus is tempted three times—rather, let us say that he is tempted for forty days—and he resists. And what temptation! How subtle, how treacherous! Mixing truth and falsehood, good and evil so adroitly that it seems impossible to separate them! Truly, this is the masterpiece of the spirit of darkness.

It is true, as we have said, that we cannot precisely equate the Lord's temptation either with Adam's or with ours, but we at least know that, through a mystery we do not seek to unravel, there was a battle within him. It was a terrible battle, one of which the anguish of Gethsemane and Golgotha can give us some impression. But what difference does the strength of the temptation make? It is enough that it was the Holy Spirit who "led" Jesus "into the wilderness to be tempted" (Matthew 4:1). God, who allows the temptation, also measures it, and you can be certain that he has taken care to strengthen his Son for the battle, giving "him whatever he needs" (Luke 11:8).

He will do the same for you, my dear friends. Therefore no temptation, past or future, should seem irresistible to you. Remember well that though it may be the devil and not God who tempts, it is God and not the devil who measures the temptation, and God measures it according to the strength that you have or that he intends for you to have.

THE EXAMPLE OF JOB

This consoling truth is clearly shown in the story of Job. Has Satan ever appeared more unleashed against a poor servant of God? Yet he always wears a chain which God lengthens or shortens at will but beyond which he can never go. The Holy Spirit lets us see the chain in this situation so we will know that Satan always has it around his neck, even when we do not see it. Satan can try nothing against Job unless he has gotten God's permission.

Satan says, "Stretch out your hand and touch all that he has" (Job 1:11). Then, in granting this to him, God sets limits in the interests of his servant. First, he protects his person. "Behold, all that he has is in your hand. Only against him do not stretch out your hand" (Job 1:12). Later, once that first temptation has strengthened Job for a harsher trial, God, again solicited by Satan, gives over his servant's person, but this time he withholds his life. "Behold, he is in your hand; only spare his life" (Job 2:6).[5]

---

[5] Note the deliberate gradation in the successive temptations Satan places before Job: loss of *fortune*, loss of *family*, loss of *health*, and, if allowed to continue, loss of *life*. A certain pride of sensitivity would probably have made us reverse that order, but "that ancient serpent:" (Revelation 12:9, 20:2) knows better than we do, and the skill of the progression he follows has the authority of God himself in this astounding story. [A.M.]

Perhaps if Job were dying in the first surprise of this new attack, he might have given in to despair and justified the insolent prediction of the adversary, "He will curse you to your face" (Job 2:5). But now he has time to get his bearings, to hear Elihu, and to humble himself before God. In spite of a few rash words, which the excess of his bitterness drags from him, he remains firm, he sends his enemy away confused, he recaptures God's favor in double measure, and he is cited in the New Testament as a model of patience (James 5:11).[6]

Console yourselves, then, my dear friends, with the thought that the devil can never tempt you without the consent of your heavenly Father nor tempt you beyond what

---

[6] One can hardly avoid feeling surprised when Saint James gives Job as an example of patience. How can we reconcile this testimony with the many bitter complaints that escape from Job beginning in the third chapter of his story? The answer is that God is more merciful in his judgments than we are. Just as one man can show more physical strength in painfully dragging a heavy weight than another would show in easily carrying a light burden, so for God the patience of his saints is measured not only in the degree of their submission but in the degree of their submission combined with the degree of their suffering. Above all, God looks into the heart, and the heart is very imperfectly revealed in the outward signs, which are all the human eye can see. Someone who utters bitter complaints may have, in the depths of his heart, more submission to God's will than someone else who is better able to control the expression of his feelings.

This last remark is confirmed by a deep study of Job's complaints. There is almost a boldness in them that one doesn't quite know how to justify; something that reveals a soul that is free before God, familiar with God, a soul that holds firm to him by virtue of an unshakeable foundation. That something honors and pleases God more than the irreproachable restraint of many others. Job's heart is explained for us by Jeremiah's heart in the words that will perhaps scandalize more than one reader but which are, I am sure, infinitely precious before God: "Righteous are you, O LORD, when I complain to you; yet I would plead my case before you" (Jeremiah 12:1). [A.M.]

your heavenly Father permits.[7] Without that authorization and beyond its limits, he can do nothing against you. Therefore never say that you are tempted beyond your strength. Under shadow of accusing the devil, you would be accusing God himself.

A PERSONAL GUARANTEE

If the historical proof I just gave is not sufficient for you, if you are asking for a formal declaration from the Lord's hand, very well, here it is, but after this be satisfied and doubt no longer. With regard to the past, it is written, "No temptation has overtaken you that is not common to man," and for the future, "God is faithful, and he will not let you be tempted beyond your ability, but with the temptation he will also provide the way of escape, that you may be able to endure it" (1 Corinthians 10:13).

What more do you need? Remember the past: "No temptation has overtaken you that is not common to man." That is to say, it is common to human nature and therefore surmountable for human nature. I am talking about human nature not as it was in Jesus, nor even as it was in Adam, but such as it is in you. If Adam before his fall or Jesus in the wilderness experienced a temptation that exceeds the strength of our nature, then that guarantees that you have been spared from it.

Beyond that, God guarantees even the future to you and guarantees it in the name of his own faithfulness: "God is faithful, and he will not let you be tempted beyond your ability, but with the temptation he will also provide the way of escape, that you may be able to endure it." Hear it well;

---

[7] The same doctrine is seen in Luke 22:31-32: "Simon, Simon, behold, Satan demanded to have you, that he might sift you like wheat, but I have prayed for you that your faith may not fail." [A.M.]

he doesn't say, "beyond Jesus' ability" or "beyond Adam's ability;" he says, "beyond your ability," your own ability.

After that, my dear brother, if you tell me, "There is a temptation that I cannot conquer, it is stronger than I am," I will have to choose—you see it yourself—between your word and God's Word, because the first affirms what the second says will never happen. No, whatever the appearances, as long as God is God and the Bible is his Word, it is impossible for us ever to be subject to a temptation that we cannot overcome.

VICTORY IN OUR GRASP

This lesson from Jesus' victory in the wilderness is frequently attested to elsewhere in Scripture and it is presupposed throughout the Bible: to yield to temptation is never a necessity. Given the need to choose among these testimonies, I will cite only a few that bear some relationship to our subject or that make some allusion to it.

PSALM 91

We find some of the clearest examples in the same Psalm 91 that Satan imprudently places in our hands and of which we would never have dreamt if it were not for the unworthy abuse he makes of it against our Master. This psalm is filled with promises of victory, but remember above all the words that immediately follow those on which Satan pretends to lean. "You will tread on the lion and the adder; the young lion and the serpent you will trample underfoot" (Psalm 91:13). Why didn't you finish your quote, cruel enemy of our souls? Isn't it because this verse relates to you?

The lion and the serpent, those two images that are twice associated with one another in a single short verse, can well indicate all the adversaries we should dread, but they

especially designate their leader, who directs and inspires
them and whom Scripture also refers to elsewhere sometimes
as a lion and sometimes as a serpent.[8] We will tread on the
lion; we will trample the serpent underfoot.

THE APOSTLES

The same assurance is given to us through the words of
the apostle, where Satan is referred to by name: "The God of
peace will soon crush Satan under your feet" (Romans 16:20).
Here Saint Paul alludes to the first prophesy, that the
woman's "offspring . . . shall bruise your head" (Genesis 3:15),
and it shows us something that a careful study of the
prophesy itself also makes evident enough: the victory is
promised not only to the Messiah, but also to the whole
family of believers.

The same doctrine is in Saint James, who doubtless has
Jesus' temptation in the wilderness in view when he writes,
"Resist the devil, and he will flee from you. Draw near to
God, and he will draw near to you" (James 4:7-8).

But all that yields to the fullness of the promises that the
Holy Spirit has given us in Saint John: "The reason the Son
of God appeared was to destroy the works of the devil. No
one born of God makes a practice of sinning, for God's seed
abides in him, and he cannot keep on sinning because he has
been born of God. By this it is evident those who are the
children of God, and those who are the children of the devil"
(1 John 3:8-10). This is not the place to expound on the
meaning of this difficult passage,[9] but it would be impossible
to deny that, at the very least, it means that God's child has
within him a secret virtue through which he can master the

---

[8] 1 Peter 5:8, 2 Timothy 4:17, Revelation 12:9 and 20:2.
[9] The word *to sin*, explained by the phrase *to practice sinning* or *to keep on
sinning*, is used here not of a brother "caught in any transgression" (Galatians 6:1), but of a heart enslaved to sin. [A.M.]

enemy and that he is never irresistibly constrained to cede him the victory.

OUR OWN EXPERIENCE

Please don't counter with your own experience. I know only too well that there is not one of our days that is not marked by some transgression. Yet whose fault is that other than ours? Please don't even counter with the experience of the least unfaithful of God's servants, of his saints, of his prophets, of his apostles. I have certainly not forgotten that, as irreproachable as their lives may be when compared with ours (Luke 1:6, 1 Thessalonians 2:10, 2 Kings 20:3, etc.), and as much as they have the incontestable right to say to us, "Be imitators of us" (see Philippians 3:17, etc.), they nevertheless have cause to say of themselves, "We all stumble in many ways" (James 3:2).[10] But is this really through a fatal and

---

[10] We are aware that there is a Christian society, known for its great works of service and great examples, that teaches that the believer can, while still on earth, attain a state in which he no longer sins. This group also points to certain disciples of Christ as having arrived, according to them, at a *perfect sanctification*. Our Wesleyan brothers appear here to have confused the *possible* with the *actual*. In principle, Scripture establishes that we are never forced to yield to temptation, but in practice it shows us not one man who never yields. In our view, it is only through faulty exegesis that someone would think he could prove that this or that saint of the Old or New Testament had attained perfection. Our *Biblical instinct* (if you will allow me that expression) would be wounded to hear it maintained that sin is ever a necessity, but it is no less wounded to hear it affirmed that this man or that woman no longer sins.

It would seem that the two points of view I attribute here to Scripture are opposed to one another. I do not think so, mainly because they are both found in God's Word. Yet I readily agree that human logic does not know exactly how to reconcile them. This is one of those numerous *antimonies* offered to us by Scripture which prevent us from reducing the Bible's teaching to a system without misunderstanding one facet of the truth and exaggerating another through our desire to be more rigorously consistent than we can be in our present condition. [A.M.]

imperious necessity? Ah, the more holy they are, the more such a thought will inspire indignation and horror in them. Go and tell Noah that he could not have helped getting drunk in his tent (Genesis 9:21). Tell Jacob that he could not have obtained the promised blessing except by lying (Genesis 27:1-29). Tell Moses that he could not have given glory to God at Meribah (Numbers 20:2-13); David that he could not have resisted Bathsheba's attractions (2 Samuel 11:2-5); Elijah that he could not have fought the discouragement of his soul (1 Kings 19:4); Hezekiah that he could not have overcome a feeling of vanity (2 Kings 20:12-19). Tell Job that he could not have withheld his unwise complaints; Zechariah that he could not have believed the angel's words (Luke 1:5-20); Saint Peter that he could not have confessed his Master in the high priest's court (Matthew 26:69-75, Mark 14:66-72, Luke 22:54-62, John 18:15-27). Tell them these things, and you will see them beating their breasts, raising their eyes toward heaven, and saying, "To you, O Lord, belongs righteousness, but to us open shame" (Daniel 9:7)!

Each time that we fall, it is our own fault. We have not been faithful in using the ever-sufficient resources that God has given us for remaining upright. Whatever the case, "Let God be true though every one were a liar" (Romans 3:4). Let his faithfulness be exonerated. "Let no one say when he is tempted, 'I am being tempted by God,' for God cannot be tempted with evil, and he himself tempts no one" (James 1:13).

My brother, my dear brother, "lift your drooping hands and strengthen your weak knees" (Hebrews 12:12). Battle courageously and confidently. You were saying, "Oh, if I were only assured of victory!" Very well, you can always be victorious in Jesus. We are not fatalists; we are Christians. Do not ever reconcile yourself with falling. Do not knowingly and voluntarily live with any sin. "Do not be overcome by evil, but overcome evil with good" (Romans 12:21).

THE VALUE OF A SINGLE VICTORY

Learn again from Jesus, victorious in the wilderness, what one single victory can mean. In the Lord's story, the wilderness temptation is one of those critical periods that determine an entire career, just as a battle won or lost can determine an entire campaign. Seen in that light, Jesus' victory not only holds Satan at bay for a time, it shatters his confidence, leaving him to return for new battles weakened through the premonition of a new defeat.

There are such decisive days for you, too. For all I know, perhaps the very day that is shining on us is one of them. Sense its full value and its full weight. If you fight valiantly, if you carry off a complete victory, you can discourage the enemy forever. But if you give ground, if you leave the result uncertain, you will embolden him and you will have him ceaselessly at your side.

"Just one more moment of weakness," you think, "one brief moment," but that is a moment chosen by the tempter for one last trial, a moment in which you will end up either ruining his hopes or reviving them. Take courage. Stand firm. Do not shrink back a single step. Do not delay for a single instant. Leave the enemy no illusion. Show him that he is wasting his time and effort with you. Through the welcome you give him, force him to recognize within the disciple the Master who defeated him in the wilderness.

It is costly to be victorious. No human enterprise demands as much resolve as the battle of faith, and it is your secret awareness of the great effort required of you that holds you back in your lethargy. Yes, but just think of the joy of triumph! Think of Job's joy once he was delivered from his trial and sanctified by it! Think of the joy of those three young men leaving their furnace (Daniel 3), or of Daniel drawn out of the lions' den (Daniel 6)! Think, above all, think of the joy of Jesus returning from his victory. Look "to Jesus, the founder and perfecter of our faith, who for the joy that was set before him[11] endured the cross, despising the shame, and is seated at the right hand of the throne of God" (Hebrews 12:2).

How great your joy also will be when you have overcome that very temptation that has previously seemed invincible to you—yes, that very one. And your joy will be all the greater because, through your victory, you can "strengthen your brothers" (Luke 22:32), just as Jesus has strengthened you through his victory! Amen.

---

[11] That is, *in order to have a share in the joy that was proposed to him as the prize for finishing the course.* [A.M.]

third meditation

THE WEAPONS

The Weapons[1]

Preparing for Battle

My dear friends,

Having been warned through Jesus' battle that a battle also waits for us, and having been reassured through his victory that we ourselves can be victorious, it only remains for us to examine in his hands the weapons through which he triumphed and through which we too can triumph.

Before beginning this subject, we would have liked to consider Jesus' preparation for battle. This would show us what we have to do so that the tempter finds us poised against his attacks, for that is half the victory. But our subject grows with study, and this discourse would then be too long, so we will limit ourselves to merely outlining the ideas.

First, let us avoid any slavish imitation that would substitute the letter for the spirit. In order to be conformed to the example of Jesus preparing for victory in the wilderness, we will not go into the wilderness to flee from temptation, and in order to conform to the example of Jesus fasting for forty days, we will not impose an annual forty-day fast on

---

[1] More than once in this meditation, I have copied, sometimes even freely translated, from a sermon by F. W. Krummacher dealing with the Lord's temptation. It is entitled *Satan's Tiefen* (Satan's depths). [A.M.]

ourselves. In so doing, one does not arm himself against temptation; he exposes himself to it. Here we should recall a principle of which an imitator of Jesus Christ must never lose sight: to imitate is not to copy.

SPIRITUAL PREPARATION

Jesus was "filled with the Holy Spirit" (Luke 1:15) after he "had been baptized and was praying" (Luke 3:21). There is the secret of his strength. Therefore, let us "pray without ceasing" (1 Thessalonians 5:17) in order to "be filled with the Spirit" (Ephesians 5:18), because to be "full of the Spirit" is also to be full of "wisdom, . . . faith, . . . and power" (Acts 6:3,5,8).

Jesus was just proclaimed by God to be his beloved Son with whom he is well pleased (Luke 3:22). As we have seen, this designation, while marking him for the attacks of the tempter, also strengthens him against those attacks by allowing him to address himself to God as to a Father who always hears him (John 11:41-42). We, too, need "the Spirit" to bear "witness with our spirit that we are children of God" (Romans 8:16), his beloved children. We will be more exposed to the enemy's assaults, but we will also be better able to resist him. "For everyone who has been born of God overcomes the world" (1 John 5:4).

Jesus is "led by the Spirit" to face temptation; he doesn't enter it of his own will. That is the source of his confidence. Where God guides, God will guard. Let us not seek danger. It cost Peter dearly to defy the warnings and force his way through (John 18:15-16),[2] entering into the very temptation to which he was foreseen to yield. Let us do our best to be

---

[2] When Jesus entered into the court of the high priest, John followed him, because he "was known to the high priest" (John 18:16), but Peter waited outside. John had to go out deliberately to speak to the servant girl who kept watch at the door so that she would let Peter enter. [A.M.]

spared from temptation, but if we cannot be spared, we will face it with the freedom of a clear conscience and with the strength born of humility.

AIDED BY PHYSICAL PREPARATION

Finally, Jesus fasts before and during the temptation. This fast, which the devil uses against Jesus, also strengthens him against the devil. The point is that Jesus fasts while praying and in order to pray. His fast is explained to us by that of Moses, who on two occasions "lay prostrate before the Lord . . . forty days and forty nights." He "neither ate bread nor drank water" (Deuteronomy 9:18, see also 9:9).

This last lesson on preparation, though abused elsewhere, is one which we have too much neglected. The use that Jesus and then his apostles made of the fast shows us a way to battle temptation—a way that is sometimes necessary. "This kind [of spirit] cannot be driven out by anything but prayer and fasting" (Mark 9:29, alternate reading). Moreover, the deprivation of food is linked to a more general fast that consists of mastering the flesh and its instincts, and that is always appropriate. "But I discipline my body and keep it under control" (1 Corinthians 9:27). "Make no provision for the flesh, to gratify its desires" (Romans 13:14).[3] Satan's point of attack is in the flesh, so when the flesh is held in check, he has nothing to lay hold of and loses his power.

THE SWORD OF THE SPIRIT

With Jesus thus prepared, let us follow him as he faces the enemy, and let us familiarize ourselves with the weapons that assure him of victory.

Jesus' weapons? Rather let us say Jesus' weapon, for he has only one: the Word of God. Tempted three times, three

---

[3] See also Luke 21:34, etc. [A.M.]

times he repels the temptation with a simple quotation from the Scriptures, without commentary or exposition. That single phrase, "It is written," works against the enemy like a dreadful volley against an attacking battalion. "It is written," and the devil retreats the first time. "It is written," and the devil retreats the second time. "It is written," and the devil withdraws.

THE WEAPON SATAN DREADS

God's Word is the weapon that Satan dreads most, a weapon before which he has always been forced to yield. It is with good reason that Saint Paul calls it "the sword of the Spirit" (Ephesians 6:17) and that Saint John in his Revelation pictures it as "a sharp two-edged sword" coming from the mouth of the Son of man (Revelation 1:16).[4] With that "sword of the Spirit" in our hand, our cause will be that of the Holy Spirit himself, and we will prevail as mightily against our adversary as God's Spirit prevails against the spirit of darkness. Without it, on the contrary, and left to ourselves, we will be as far beneath him as human nature is beneath that of the angels. Adam only succumbed because he let that sword fall; Jesus triumphed because nothing could wrench it from his hands.

But how is it that the Son of God, instead of going against the enemy with some new sword brought down with him from heaven, chooses to arm himself only with our sword, picked up on this old earth where Adam left it, carelessly forgotten? The answer is that Jesus must serve as an example for us; we need to learn what the sword can do in our hands by what it does in his hands. Therefore let us, in

---

[4] See also Revelation 2:16, 19:15,21. Similarly, Hebrews 4:12 says, "The word of God is living and active, sharper than any two-edged sword, piercing to the division of soul and of spirit, of joints and of marrow, and discerning the thoughts and intentions of the heart." [A.M.]

turn, raise it up—or rather let us receive it from him as freshly tempered by his victory—and we will have nothing to fear. Let us oppose every attack of the adversary with a simple *it is written*, and we will render all his efforts vain.

THE POWER OF *IT IS WRITTEN*

The devil would like to reengage you with the world. He works at it cleverly. He slides up next to you and points out to you that it is hardly in line with charity to hold yourself so far removed from human society. He suggests that you will be better able to win men to the Gospel by frequenting their amusements, thus showing them that you do not advocate religion in the sense of the anchorites.[5] Finally, he tells you that too much caution is unbecoming for one who is training himself in Christian virtue, and that in overcoming without risk one triumphs without glory. Thus says the tempter. If you defend yourself only with your own reason, you will be all the more easily persuaded, because your natural heart is in far too much agreement with his arguments. But if you arm yourself with God's Word, if you respond in faith, "It is written, 'Do not be conformed to this world'" (Romans 12:2), then this single word puts everything in its place, the adversary is unmasked, and his malice is defeated.

The devil wants to remove from your spirit the idea that the Christian faith is the only way of salvation. He leads you to some vast square in a large city and shows you the throngs of people ceaselessly moving to and fro, one after the other. Then he says to you, "Do you really believe that all these people are on their way to perdition? Surely, your heart and your reason cannot accept such a doctrine. Yet most of these people don't believe in Jesus Christ, or at the very least they

---

[5] Those who withdraw from secular society for religious reasons, often in order to focus intensely on prayer or to lead an ascetic life.

don't believe the way you and those like you do. Could it really be true that your little path is the only one in the world that leads to eternal life? Aren't your views here rather narrow and unworthy of God?" Thus reasons the tempter. If you resist him only in your own wisdom, you will not last very long against him, and at the end of the encounter you will sense yourself to be uncertain, wavering, and cold. But if you take God's Word in your hand, if you reply without hesitation, "It is written, 'I am the way, and the truth, and the life. No one comes to the Father except through me'" (John 14:6), then the spell is shattered, "the snare is broken, and [you] have escaped" from the hand of the treacherous fowler (Psalm 124:7).

Or yet again, the devil wants to rob a faithful minister of Jesus Christ of the vigor of his preaching. He counsels the minister not to appear so intractable, not to cry heresy for so little cause, not to make heaven so stingy and salvation so difficult, and not to sadden the good news of grace with fanciful ideas of a devil or hell. He contends that greater tractability would gain the minister the good graces of all his listeners, thus permitting him to lead them more surely to faith and to make more fruitful use of the good gifts that heaven has granted him. Thus counsels the tempter. If you rely only on your own light in order to refute him, you will surely fall into his trap, for he is very clever at making "evil good and good evil," or putting "darkness for light and light for darkness" (Isaiah 5:20). But if you lean on God's Word, if you reply with confidence, "It is written, 'If anyone is preaching to you a gospel contrary to the one you received, let him be accursed'" (Galatians 1:9), then "the strong man" has found "one stronger than he" (Luke 11:21-22), and there is nothing left for him but to quit the battlefield in shame.

Oh, if we but knew what the Word of God can do, and what it can do in our own hands! If we but knew the terror it inspires in our formidable adversary, even as he pretends to laugh at it in our presence, so as to make us loosen our grip! If, after hearing him mock God's Word on temptation's stage, we could—so to speak—but follow him behind the scenes and hear him confess to his accomplices that he is lost unless he can make this irresistible weapon fall from our hands! If we but knew all that and, like the valiant Eleazar, held on firmly until our "hand was weary and . . . clung to the sword" (2 Samuel 23:10), oh, then we would be invincible; yes, invincible!

THE SOURCE OF THAT POWER

But for that Word of God to have in our hands the same power that it had in Jesus' hands, it must be for us all that it was for him. I know of nothing in the entire history of humanity or even in the field of divine revelations that speaks more clearly than our text in favor of the inspiration of the Scriptures.

What! The Son of God, "who is in the bosom of the Father" (John 1:18, literal reading) and who can so easily draw on his own inner resources, prefers to borrow what he needs from the book he finds in our hands and to find his strength where Joshua, Samuel, and David found theirs!

What! Jesus Christ, the king of heaven and earth, calls on Moses his servant to help him in this solemn hour! The one "who comes from heaven" and "bears witness to what he has seen and heard" strengthens himself against the temptations of hell using the word of him who "speaks in an earthly way" (John 3:32,31, see also Hebrews 12:25)!

How can we explain this astonishing mystery, this prodigious reversal unless the word of Moses was for Jesus "not . . . the word of men but . . . the word of God" (1 Thessalonians 2:13)? How can we explain it unless he was fully persuaded that the holy "men spoke from God as they were carried along by the Holy Spirit" (2 Peter 1:21)?

DIVINE INSPIRATION

I am not forgetting, my dear friends (and here I am especially speaking to the young servants of the Word), the objections that the inspiration of the Scriptures has raised, nor the real obscurities with which it is shrouded. If they sometimes trouble your hearts, they have also troubled mine. But when that has happened I have only had to cast a glance at Jesus glorifying the Scriptures in the wilderness in order to strengthen my faith, and I have seen the most embarrassing problems transformed into historical fact, palpable, appealing to the eye for whoever is willing to rely on Christ. Jesus was, no doubt, not ignorant of the difficulties of inspiration, and the portion of the Scriptures that he cites, the Old Testament, is the one that offers the greatest number of them. Did that prevent him from invoking their testimony with boundless confidence? May what sufficed for him, suffice for you. Do not fear that this rock, which supported your Savior's hand in the hour of his temptation and distress, will give way beneath your hand because you leaned on it too hard.

What is it that preoccupies you about inspiration? Is it the variations between different manuscripts? Apart from a perpetual miracle, such variations are inevitable, and some already existed in Jesus' day in the Old Testament from which he quotes here three times.

Is it the small divergences among the sacred authors in their descriptions of the same event, such as those that are found between Saint Matthew and Saint Luke in the very story that serves as our text?[6] Divergences at least as great as these existed between books of the Old Testament, for example between Kings and Chronicles.

---

[6] Differences in the quotation from Deuteronomy 8:3 (Matthew 4:4 vs. Luke 4:4) and in the order of the temptations. [A.M.]

Is it the degrees of inspiration? Are you afraid that there is less inspiration in the historical books than in the prophetic ones? Jesus always cites Scripture as an authority that "cannot be broken" (John 10:35), and in the place that concerns us, his quotations are all drawn from a historical book, Deuteronomy.

Finally, are you puzzled about what theory of inspiration to adopt: what is its mode and extent, what part does it leave as man's contribution, does it direct the sacred author's spirit or his pen, and other questions of a similar nature? Here again, follow Jesus' example. On all of these speculative questions, he offers no explanation. But is it a matter of the practical question? Is it a matter of the confidence with which you can quote the Scriptures, all of the Scriptures, even down to a single phrase of the Scriptures? It is impossible to be clearer, firmer, or more positive than Jesus is.[7] Go and do likewise. Quote the Scriptures as Jesus did, and have whatever theory you would like on inspiration.

Jesus has a vantage point more elevated and more disengaged from earthly influences than that of our theology. Let us follow him onto these heights where one breathes an atmosphere that is so pure and luminous, and where the haze with which earth obscures heavenly truth stops below our feet.[8] Ah, when the devil comes to throw into your spirit another one of those school-room subtleties that he always keeps in reserve against the inspiration of the Scriptures, be content to send him to Jesus, saying, "Why didn't you say all

---

[7] Jesus' quotations prove this only for the Old Testament. The inspiration of the New Testament has its own proofs and rests equally, though in a different way, on the authority of Jesus Christ. Moreover, there are no men except the Jews who receive the inspiration of the Old Testament while rejecting that of the New. [A.M.]

[8] "Eat in peace the bread of the Scriptures, without worrying about the grain of sand the millstone might have mixed in there." (Letter of Bengel to a young theologian) [A.M.]

that to my Master when he fended you off in the wilderness using that Word which seems so weak and uncertain to you? Go, take your objections to him, and when they have shaken him, they will shake me also!"

WIELDING THE SWORD

Jesus has no other weapon against Satan than God's Word, but how does he wield that weapon? Let us study each of the three quotations that he successively borrows from the Scriptures. Thus his example, which has just revealed to us the power of God's Word, will also teach us how we should use it.

After forty days and forty nights spent in the wilderness, Jesus experiences a sense of hunger which he seems to have been spared during the course of his fast. All this is supernatural. It is then that the devil approaches and begins to attack him. We have had occasion elsewhere to contemplate the three temptations in the wilderness through what could be called their external side, that is to say through the objects to which they relate: "the desires of the flesh and the desires of the eyes and pride in possessions" (1 John 2:16). Here we look at them from their internal side. By this I mean the attitude through which the devil was hoping to make the Lord yield and which really constitutes the spirit of the temptation. Looked at in this way, the first temptation is a temptation to distrust, the second a temptation to unfaithfulness, and the third a temptation to presumption.

THE TEMPTATION TO DISTRUST

The devil begins, "If you are the Son of God, command this stone to become bread." The moment is well chosen, the temptation subtle. The tempter wants Jesus to take the divine virtue with which he, as Messiah, is clothed and turn it to his personal advantage. Satan does so by implying that Jesus is the Messiah, while perhaps also wanting to make him doubt this fact. It is as if he said, "Use the means at your disposal to provide for your own needs, instead of relying on God, whom you call your Father but who seems to have forgotten you."

If Jesus gave in to that proposition, which hid such a treacherous core beneath such well-meaning appearances, he would leave God's paths through having doubted God's help. He would be using his power, as Satan had done, for his own satisfaction, and the work of redemption would be ruined at the outset. But Jesus, without hesitation, repels the enemy with this testimony from the Scriptures as his only response: "Man shall not live by bread alone, but by every word that comes from the mouth of God" (Matthew 4:3; Deuteronomy 8:3).[9] This quotation perhaps seems strange to you and not well suited to the circumstances, but you will no longer think so when you have penetrated its meaning.

WHY DEUTERONOMY?

The quotation is taken from Deuteronomy and is drawn from the story of the people of Israel in the wilderness. Note that the other two answers given by Jesus Christ to the tempter are also borrowed from the same story and the same book. How is it that Jesus, with the full range of the Scriptures open before him, takes his stand against the enemy in this one place, as in an impregnable fortress? It is because he recognizes a secret relationship between himself, the Son of God paving the way for the foundation of his kingdom with forty days of fasting and temptation in the Judean wilderness, and Israel, that other Son of God (Hosea 11:1) being

---

[9] Jesus, who here refuses to use his power to meet his own needs, uses it elsewhere to obtain an overabundance for others (see John 2:1-11). [A.M.]

prepared for the conquest of Canaan with forty years of privations and trials in the great Arabian Desert.

Israel, which is presented to us as a type for the New-Testament church, is also a type for Jesus, the head of that church and the one in whom it is fully embodied. That is why Jesus instructs and strengthens himself through what is written for Israel. What a wonderful progression of the Scriptures! What marvelous unity of spirit between the two Testaments!

THE WORD THAT FEEDS

Moses said to the people of Israel, "He humbled you and let you hunger and fed you with manna, which you did not know, nor did your fathers know, that he might make you know that man does not live by bread alone, but man lives by all that comes from the mouth of the LORD" (Deuteronomy 8:3, literal reading), or, as our text puts it, "by every word of God." [10]

Bread is not the only thing God has at his disposal as the ordinary means for nourishing humanity, for the secret of its nutritional value resides not in the bread but in God's word, from which alone every virtue and every blessing flow. Bread is only assimilated into the substance of our bodies because God's word said at the beginning, "Behold, I have given you every plant yielding seed that is on the face of all the earth. . . . You shall have them for food" (Genesis 1:29). If, instead of pronouncing that blessing on wheat, the same word had been pronounced over wood or stone, the wood or

---

[10] The Bible Monod was using follows some original manuscripts by including the phrase "by every word of God" in Luke's account of the temptation, thus giving a fuller quotation from Deuteronomy 8:3. Most newer translations of the Bible omit this phrase, though it is given in Matthew's account.

stone would nourish us just as well as wheat does. This would be no stranger a sight than the wood sweetening the waters of Marah (Exodus 15:23-25) or the rock giving water to Israel for their thirst (Exodus 17:1-6; 1 Corinthians 10:4).

Without God's word, bread itself would be unable to nourish anyone, and you would "eat, but . . . never have enough" (Haggai 1:6). On the other hand, without bread, God's word can nourish whomever it wants, however it wants. God demonstrated this with Moses' companions by nourishing them for forty years with manna—manna that ceased falling on the day they set foot on cultivated soil (Joshua 5:12). Beyond that, God's word can sustain man's body without bread, without manna, without visible means of any kind. On two occasions, Moses lived for forty days on Mount Sinai and "neither ate bread nor drank water" (Deuteronomy 9:9,18). Elijah walked without eating or drinking, also for forty days, toward the same mountain across the same desert. Jesus, in turn, led by his Father's will into a solitude where everything is lacking, is sustained so marvelously during his forty day fast that he doesn't even suffer hunger. Through it all, he counts on the one who had him come into the wilderness to make him also live in the wilderness. He willingly leaves the choice of means to his Father's wisdom, having learned from Moses that "man does not live by bread alone, but man lives by every word that comes from the mouth of God" (Deuteronomy 8:3). No sooner has that Scripture, taken in its deep and intimate sense, been quoted than it overturns every effort of the enemy and sets at naught his first attack.

My dear friends, each time that the tempter pushes you to doubt God's help because ordinary means have failed you, answer as Jesus did, "Man does not live by bread alone, but by every word of God."

DISTRUST FOR MATERIAL NEEDS

Perhaps up to now you have painfully earned bread for you and your family, but suddenly you are out of work or your strength is gone or your usual resources have vanished.

This is a "time" of which the devil will not neglect to make "the best use" (Ephesians 5:16). He would not dare to suggest that you deceive or steal, but he will say to you, "Doesn't God, your Father, have some better feast for you than these stones and thistles among which he leaves you to vegetate? All right, since he has abandoned you, help yourself. Don't be afraid to stray a little from the beaten paths and to provide for your needs through one of those expedients about which you have had too many scruples. Get involved in that speculation; try the shining luck of gambling; be less difficult in choosing your relationships; flatter unscrupulously those whose protection you need." In other words, "Command this stone to become bread."

Answer him, "Man shall not live by bread alone, but by every word of God." " 'My God whom I serve is able to deliver me, . . . and he will deliver me, . . . but if not' (see Daniel 3:17-18), I will in no way stray from his paths, and though I must die of hunger, I want to 'abstain from every form of evil' " (1 Thessalonians 5:22).

DISTRUST FOR SPIRITUAL NEEDS

Food for your soul gives rise to similar temptations, which you will fend off in the same spirit. Perhaps you find yourself relegated to spiritual solitude, kept in a place where your heart "longs, yes, faints for the courts of the Lord" (Psalm 84:2) and for the fellowship of his people. Perhaps you are bound to a position or to a society where everything opposes your growth in grace (2 Peter 3:18). For you, the pathway of sanctification bristles with temptations and obstacles. But this solitude was made for you by God. This position was chosen for you by God, and you cannot leave it without violating pressing obligations. This society is your natural family, and God has commanded you to take care of it, or else you will have "denied the faith and [been] worse than an unbeliever" (1 Timothy 5:8).

In such moments, the devil will say to you, "Isn't it time to provide deliverance for your soul? Stop, at all costs, a state of affairs that makes the Christian life impossible for you." "Command this stone to become bread."

Answer him, "Man shall not live by bread alone, but by every word of God." "Blessing comes from God, and that blessing isn't attached to any particular human condition. I am where God wants me, and that is enough for me. He who at will 'turns . . . a fruitful land into a salty waste' and 'a desert into pools of water' (Psalm 107:34-35) is also he who can change the most terrible temptations into precious means of grace. He is able to keep me in all my ways except in the way of disobedience."

DISTRUST FOR A PASTOR'S NEEDS

Perhaps you are a servant of God who, through the Lord's visible dispensations, has been placed at the head of a church where singular blessings have not ceased to confirm your calling. But the church is poor, and you yourself are poor. At the beginning of the year, you don't know how you will provide for the expenses that each of the next three hundred and sixty-five days will bring. Dear brother, there you are, truly in the wilderness, but in a wilderness where God has led you as if by the hand.

Then the devil says to you, "The God whom you serve so faithfully has forsaken you. During all the years that you have been bringing him requests for yourself and your household, what has he done to relieve your righteous concern? What are you waiting for? Leave such a thankless position. Seek some other job, one that will 'give you your bread and your water, your wool and your flax, your oil and your drink' (see Hosea 2:5)." "Command this stone to become bread."

Answer him, "Man shall not live by bread alone, but by every word of God." "God, who is faithful toward those who are faithful, has the resources ready for all my needs. Wherever he has sent me, he has never left me lacking anything.[11] As long as I am convinced that this is the place to which he has assigned me, I will stay here and 'wait quietly for the salvation of the LORD' (Lamentations 3:26)."

Answer in that way, my friends, and God will help you. Many of your brothers have been visited as you are. They waited for the Lord, and now that God has shown them "the salvation" promised to the "one who orders his way rightly" (Psalm 50:23), they would not trade the lessons learned in their distress for all the gold in the world.[12]

THE TEMPTATION TO UNFAITHFULNESS

The first temptation has been overcome, and overcome by the Word of God. The devil resorts to another. "And the devil took him up and showed him all the kingdoms of the world in a moment of time, and said to him, 'To you I will give all this authority and their glory, for it has been delivered to me, and I give it to whom I will. If you, then, will worship me, it will all be yours.'"

---

[11] "When I sent you out with no moneybag or knapsack or sandals, did you lack anything?" They said, "Nothing" (Luke 22:35). [A.M.]

[12] Perhaps there is a word of personal testimony here. Early in Monod's career, after he was discharged from the prominent but worldly Reformed Church of Lyons, a number of evangelical Christians, mostly poor, who had already left the church, asked him to become their pastor. He did so, thus founding an independent evangelical congregation which flourished and with which he maintained close and warm relations until his death, long after he had ceased to be its pastor.

How does this mysterious scene take place? We don't know. As I said, I take my text's narrative as a child. Without seeking to probe "the secret things" that "belong to the LORD our God," I go directly to "the things that are revealed" and that "belong to us and to our children" (Deuteronomy 29:29). There is much to learn here about the wiles of the adversary and about what we must do to escape from them.

SATAN'S AUTHORITY

What should we think about Satan's statement, "it has been delivered to me, and I give it to whom I will"? As with all of the adversary's seductions, it is a mixture of truth and falsehood. If everything were true, "the father of lies" (John 8:44) would find no advantage in it, whereas if all were falsehood, his game would too easily be discovered. It is all too true that Satan exerts a prodigious influence in the world, an influence that he holds because of sin and that he places in the service of sin. He usurped it in Eden where, not content to lay hold of man's spirit, we see this king of the earth putting himself in the place of the very King of heaven as the object for man's obedience.

We need only look around us to recognize the deadly rights that the enemy has acquired over us. History, politics, science, the arts, literature—every variety of glory and beauty gives all too striking testimony to it. Moreover, Scripture calls Satan "the ruler of this world" (John 12:31) because of his power, and even calls him (oh disgrace!) "the god of this world" (2 Corinthians 4:4) because he is so much worshiped. But Satan's power, such as it is, "has been delivered to" him, as he himself is forced to confess, and having been delivered to him, it is not absolute; it is exercised under the control of God, who causes it to serve the final fulfillment of his plans. If Satan is the ruler of this world, only God is "the Most

High," who "rules the kingdom of men and gives it to whom he will" (Daniel 4:17). Then too, having been delivered to him, Satan's power is not eternal. It rests on sin, and when sin is abolished, his power will be withdrawn. In fact, it was to abolish sin that the Messiah came, having "appeared" in order "to destroy the works of the devil" (1 John 3:8) and to establish a new "kingdom that shall never be destroyed" (Daniel 2:44) on the ruins of his empire. Thus what Satan here dares to attribute to himself, what he pretends to sell to God's Son, really belongs to the Son, to whom the Father promised, "I will make the nations your heritage, the ends of the earth your possession" (Psalm 2:8).

THE GOD OF THIS AGE

Whatever the case, Satan offers Jesus what he has at his disposal and perhaps also what he does not have. He causes "all the kingdoms of the world . . . and their glory" to pass before his eyes—the pride of power, the dazzle of riches, the splendor of luxury, the vanity of honors, the allurement of pleasures, and all of that earthly pomp that so inflames man's covetousness. Then he says, " 'It will all be yours,' on the one condition that 'you . . . worship me.' " In other words, instead of waiting and conquering the inheritance promised by the Father, Jesus is to take it right away and without a struggle from Satan's hand by giving him the homage that is due to God alone.

That is the spirit of the second temptation, and it has something more shocking about it than the first. That condition to which rule in the world is attached is nothing less than a pact with the devil. Thus on hearing this impious proposal, Jesus abandons for a moment the serenity that characterizes his resistance.[13] Calling Satan by name for the

---

[13] See Jude 9. [A.M.]

first time, he repels him with holy indignation: "Be gone, Satan! For it is written, 'You shall worship the Lord your God and him only shall you serve' " (Matthew 4:10).[14] That quotation stops the enemy's efforts immediately and sends him away defeated for the second time.

Here things are so clear, Satan's proposal is so detestable, and Jesus' response is so simple that explanations would be superfluous, but the applications will not be. However detestable the temptation might have been, God's children are all exposed to it, and however simple the response might have been, we must always know how to find it. There is not one of us to whom an alliance with Satan has not been offered more than once. That is what I call the tacit agreement through which a man undertakes to serve the god of this world in order to obtain the favor of this world; it is the agreement through which a Christian perhaps agrees to give homage to Satan in order to assure himself, in his impatience, of "the glory that comes from man" instead of pursuing by faith "the glory that comes from God" alone (John 12:43). Let us give a few examples borrowed from the experiences of youth.

THE LURE OF RICHES

The most common form under which Satan proposes his dreadful alliance is the coveting of riches. A young man, moral and godly, has just entered a career in business. The hope of making a brilliant fortune captures his spirit, but how to realize that hope? Among the means presented to him are some that are common in the world but are the means of sin: lying, deceiving, harming a neighbor, initiating lawsuits, dividing families, neglecting God's service, violating the day

---

[14] These words are borrowed from Deuteronomy 6:13 in the Septuagint, which reproduces Moses' thought without adhering exactly to the words he uses. [A.M.]

of rest. This is the devil saying to you, "All these I will give you, if you will fall down and worship me" (Matthew 4:9), and, alas, there are few fortunes that have been made without concessions to Satan!

Answer him, my young brother, "Be gone, Satan! For it is written, 'You shall worship the Lord your God and him only shall you serve'" (Matthew 4:10). Let Satan keep all his advantages, since he values them so highly. Do not beg the devil for the deceitful image of a glory that God will give you in reality if you are faithful. Moreover, even down here, blessing comes from God. "Godliness . . . holds promise for the present life and also for the life to come" (1 Timothy 4:8).

THE LURE OF MARRIAGE

Sometimes Satan's alliance is disguised under a proposal of marriage. A young woman was walking faithfully in the Lord's ways. Through her fervent yet modest godliness, she was an example to her companions, an honor to the church, and a source of edification to the world. Her hand is sought by a young man having everything in his favor—fortune, rank, spirit. He is amiable, perhaps loved . . . but a stranger to godliness and one to whom she could unite herself only to the detriment of her faith. This is Satan saying to you, "All this I will give you, if you will fall down and worship me." "See what a future is set before you; what honor, what joy, what love! Would you want to deprive yourself of all that? And why? For the sad pleasure of leading an austere and depressing life? Keep your faith—you can do it!—just keep it closed up in your heart. Be of the world while you are in the world."

How could a weak child resist a tactic of the adversary so deceitfully conceived? Through that simple word, "Be gone, Satan! For it is written, 'You shall worship the Lord your

God and him only shall you serve.' " Yes, my young sister, answer him in that way, and, behold, you are victorious. Moreover, the Lord's "grace is sufficient for you" (2 Corinthians 12:9). Go and gently lay at the foot of the cross all those prospects of happiness of which your poor heart has dreamed, and in his love you will find something to repay with interest all your sacrifices.

THE LURE OF PROMINENT MINISTRY

The sanctuary provides no shelter from Satan's offers of alliance. A young minister enters the service of the church, endowed with the finest of God's gifts. He can aspire to the world's glory, to the accolades of men, to the best-paid and most influential places, but to get there, he must subscribe to the doctrines of the age, or accommodate the truth to its sensibilities, or take part in the frivolity of its pleasures, or make common cause with it against the children of God. This again is Satan saying to you, "All this I will give you, if you will fall down and worship me," and how many young ministers perhaps give in to that temptation! How many, like Demas, have abandoned their brothers, being "in love with this present world" (2 Timothy 4:10)! How many, like the priests, have "believed in [Jesus], but . . . they did not confess it . . . for they loved the glory that comes from man more than the glory that comes from God" (John 12:42-43)!

Oh my young friends, be faithful, be unshakeable. Reply, "Be gone, Satan! For it is written, 'You shall worship the Lord your God and him only shall you serve.' " If you are still trying to please man, you are not a servant of Christ (see Galatians 1:10). Confess Jesus Christ as your God, his Word as your rule, and his people as your people, and "when the chief Shepherd appears, you will receive the unfading crown of glory" (1 Peter 5:4)!

THE TEMPTATION TO PRESUMPTION

Defeated twice, Satan makes one last attempt, for which one can anticipate that he will gather all of his cunning and resources. "He took him to Jerusalem and set him on the pinnacle of the temple and said to him, 'If you are the Son of God, throw yourself down from here, for it is written, "He will command his angels concerning you, to guard you," and "on their hands they will bear you up, lest you strike your foot against a stone" ' " (Psalm 91:11-12).

DISTORTED CONFIDENCE

To really understand this temptation, we need to set it against the first, with which it offers an obvious contrast. The tempter has sought in vain to make Jesus doubt his Father. This method, commonly his first recourse and one which succeeded all too well with Eve, ran aground against Jesus' unshakeable confidence in God's help. Now the tempter conceives the hope of seducing him through that very confidence, but through a distortion of that confidence. He "disguises himself as an angel of light" (2 Corinthians 11:14); he surrounds himself with holy things; he leads Jesus into the holy city, places him on the pinnacle of the holy temple, and encourages him by the holy Word of God to throw himself down without fear from its height, in order to give the crowd a striking token of who he is through the marvel of the promised protection.

Yes, but is the risky action that Satan proposes to Jesus really necessary? Is it what God wants? Does it meet the required conditions for the promise of Psalm 91 to be applicable? If Jesus yielded to the tempter's suggestion, he would be engaging his Father's faithfulness without warrant; he would be making God's Word into an amusement rather than a support; he would be creating risk for the frivolous satisfaction of provoking deliverance. And if that deliverance were lacking, he would jeopardize the glory of God through his blind and presumptuous confidence just as much as he would have served that glory through humble and obedient faith. Thus he responds without hesitation to his treacherous counselor, "It is said, 'You shall not tempt the LORD your God' " (see Deuteronomy 6:16 KJV).

TEMPTING GOD

What does it mean to "tempt God," and how would Jesus have tempted God in throwing himself down from the height of the temple? To "tempt God" or "test God" [15] is, as the natural sense of the words indicates, to put God to the test and thus to try his faithfulness. Faith, on the other hand, simply counts on God and leans on his faithfulness as on an immoveable rock. Faith speaks thus: "Has he said, and will he not do it?" (Numbers 23:19), and it demands no other token of God's promise than the promise itself. The one who tempts God uses completely different language. "Will God? Does God want to? Can God?" Then, led by the need to clarify his doubt, he allows himself to prescribe certain conditions that he wants to see God fulfill before resting on his promise.

The Israelites "tested the LORD" at Rephidim by asking for water to drink and by asking for it in the spirit of determining, based on the reception given to their demand, "Is the LORD among us or not?" (Exodus 17:7). They tempted him again at Kibroth-hattaavah, asking for new food. "He struck the rock so that water gushed out and streams overflowed. Can he also give bread or provide meat for his people?" (Psalm 78:19-20, see Numbers 11).

---

[15] "Your fathers put me to the test and saw my works for forty years" (Hebrews 3:9-10). The thought of this verse is, "Your fathers wanted to put my power to the test. Very well, I made them acquainted with it, but by deploying it against them." See also Isaiah 7:12 and Acts 5:9. [A.M.]

The same spirit in less crude forms reappears in the Christian church. Those new disciples who opposed the apostles in the council of Jerusalem tempted God by wanting to burden the converted pagans with a yoke that they themselves were unable to bear,[16] thereby seeming to impose on God an extraordinary outpouring of grace which they had no right to expect. This conduct was all the more reprehensible in that if the Lord, thus provoked,[17] chose to refuse the conditions they dared to prescribe for him, his character or his word would appear to be at fault. False confidence and distrust, presumption and unbelief touch each other. They have a single principle and similar results.

Jesus, in turn, would have tempted God if he had thrown himself down from the height of the temple. Having for such a strange act neither command nor necessity, he could not say, "God will protect me," but at most, "Will God protect me? Will he be able to bring me safe and sound to the ground? Let's try it." If he said that even once, he would be defeated, but his refusal, his quotation of the Scriptures, "You shall not put the Lord your God to the test," upsets the adversary's plan and puts him to flight for the third and final time.

My brothers, Satan can also tempt us to tempt God. Examples abound; the only problem is which ones to choose.

RESOURCES FOR MINISTRY

"The silver is mine, and the gold is mine, declares the LORD of hosts" (Haggai 2:8). In an enterprise formed for the Lord's glory and carried out in his Spirit, we can expect the Lord to furnish the necessary resources. He will not

---

[16] They wanted the converted pagans to accept circumcision and obey the law of Moses (see Acts 15:4-11).

[17] "They tempted the strong God, and provoked the Holy One of Israel" (Psalm 78:51, literal translation). [A.M.]

confound our faith. By the same token, without that faith, the finest works of charity and of Christian godliness would have been halted at the outset. The likes of Francke,[18] Cotolingo,[19] and Marie Calame would have failed in their mission. But avoid going off, under pretext of confidence in God, to throw yourself with rash assurance into the first pathway that opens before you.

Here again, you will certainly not be spared Satan's suggestions. Sometimes he will incite you to take as an inspiration of God's Spirit a project that, in spite of good appearances, tends less to his glory than to yours. Sometimes, as you are executing a project approved by God, he will incite you to make expenditures that are neither demanded by necessity nor in conformity with gospel simplicity. Sometimes he will urge you to run impatiently ahead of God's timing and thus disturb the slow and sure progress by which God loves to guarantee the success of a cause, even as he exercises the humility of the instrument.

"What are you afraid of, man of little faith?" Satan will say to you. "Commit yourself in the Lord's name. Give, promise, buy, build, do everything you find at hand. If you are a child of God, trust your Father." In other words, "Throw yourself down from here." If you listen to him, you will find yourself imperceptibly drawn into obligations for which you are inadequate. Then the gospel will be compromised in the eyes of the world, which, on seeing your uncompleted projects, will say "This man began to build and was not able to finish" (Luke 14:30). Meanwhile you yourself will perhaps

---

[18] Auguste Hermann Francke (1663-1727) was a German pietist, theologian, and philanthropist who established two schools for the education of the poor and a printing house to make inexpensive copies of the Bible available.

[19] Giuseppe Benedetto Cottolengo (1786-1842), in addition to founding a number of Roman Catholic religious orders, also established the Little House of Divine Providence in Turin to house poor people.

be delivered over to financial concerns that will break your heart, even if they do not shake your faith.

Avoid such a great evil by walking scrupulously with God, tempering the freedom of Christ with the prudence of Christ, and leaving the beaten path only to respond to an obvious calling or to obey a clear leading of the Spirit. That is the secret of prayer. Apart from that, "You shall not put the Lord your God to the test." There is your reply; there is your rest.

AN EDUCATION

Fathers and mothers, it is you who will furnish my second example, so listen especially carefully. The moment seems to have come to send your son or daughter away from the family home and to avail yourselves of a boarding school[20] either to complete his instruction or to form his spirit and character. But what principles will govern the serious and difficult choice of that second family that you are going to substitute for your child's natural family? If your first consideration is "the one thing . . . necessary" (Luke 10:42), you will prove the truth of the promise, "Seek first the kingdom of God and his righteousness, and all these things will be added to you" (Matthew 6:33). But if, too preoccupied with the glory that comes from men, you seek for your son primarily the means to distinguish himself in the world, and for your daughter the means to please it; if you place your child for these years in a setting where the name of Jesus Christ is neither honored nor loved nor perhaps even known; worse than that, if you deliver this trusting soul and this impressionable spirit over to the influence of a blind,

---

[20] Literally "public education." The context suggests private boarding schools rather than the government-run local schools one thinks of today. In Monod's day, much of the education was done in the home by parents and tutors and so was considered "private."

opinionated proselytism, whose scruples (if it had any) your negligence seems intended to disarm, then what will you have done but tempt God?

Consider then the voice that says to you softly, "Aren't the advantages of a brilliant education worth a few sacrifices? Can God not preserve your child from the contagion of error or the influence of examples? Can you only win him to godliness by harassing him with Bible in hand?" Whose voice is that but the voice of the one who said to Jesus, "Throw yourself down from here"? And what reply do you have to give him other than Jesus' reply, "You shall not put the Lord your God to the test"?

Alas, how many parents I could name who weep bitter tears over the sin and folly of having counted on God to remove their children from the perils to which they had subjected them without God's consent.

OTHER DANGEROUS ALLUREMENTS

At another time, the tempter will push you to frequent questionable company, because God can protect you from their influence. Or he will tempt you to waste your inner life in frivolous, if not corrupting reading, because God can defend you against its assaults. Or he will encourage you to follow the intellectuals who proclaim dangerous novelties, because God can close your heart to the seduction of their discourses.

There are so many variants of his counsel to Jesus, "Throw yourself down from here," and to each of these you must respond, "It is written, 'You shall not put the Lord your God to the test.' "

In the perils to which it pleases God to expose you, be firm and unshakeable, but do not create any dangers for yourself. Never put God to the test, do not put his glory on the line, and should you be placed on the pinnacle of the temple, do not throw yourself down but descend calmly and humbly by the building's staircase.

SATAN'S USE OF SCRIPTURE

There is another aspect of this last temptation that merits our particular attention: the use that Satan makes of the Scriptures. He saw that Jesus twice used them to fend him off, so he forms the audacious plan of turning that sword of the Holy Spirit, whose irresistible power he has just experienced, against his conqueror. What marvelous skill on the part of the tempter, who makes use of everything and who, arming himself against us with our own resources, seeks to weaken us through our strength just as God strengthens us through our weakness! "Throw yourself down from here, for it is written, 'He will command his angels concerning you, to guard you,' and 'on their hands they will bear you up, lest you strike your foot against a stone.' "

SCRIPTURE MUST INTERPRET SCRIPTURE

Where does the treachery of that quotation lie? To that question, many reply that Satan has maliciously shortened the passage he cites. The psalmist said, "He will command his angels concerning you to guard you *in all your ways*" (Psalm 91:11), and those last words, which the tempter omits, make it clear that we can only count on the promised help by remaining in the paths of our calling. That remark appears subtle to me. Besides, it seems that if it were correct, Jesus would have responded by reestablishing the integrity of the mutilated text.

No, Satan does not alter the terms of the passage he quotes, but he makes a false application. The help that is guaranteed in Psalm 91 has its set conditions, conditions from which Jesus would stray by throwing himself off the height of the temple. God wanted to reassure those of his children who find themselves inevitably exposed to peril, not those who precipitate themselves there by choice and without obligation. But since that restriction isn't found in the psalmist's expressions, how will Jesus prove that it is part of the Holy Spirit's thought? Will it be by appealing to his own reason or to natural sentiment? No, it will be in appealing to Scripture itself.

Jesus doesn't answer, "The meaning you are giving to that verse of Scripture cannot be right because it is too strange." He answers, "This meaning cannot be right because it contradicts another verse of Scripture." The Lord's intention is even clearer in Saint Matthew's account, which adds to Saint Luke's account the word *again*, which is highly significant here. "Again it is written, 'You shall not put the Lord your God to the test' " (Matthew 4:7). In other words, you need to combine these two testimonies, which complement and explain one another; Jesus has the right to count on angelic intervention only if he is not putting God to the test.

This is highly instructive. The Bible is written not by philosophers for philosophers but by simple men for simple men. It contains places that need clarification and which, if not well understood, can furnish weapons against us to the tempter. These clarifications must be sought not in human wisdom but in Scripture speaking someplace else.

Moreover, if one permits human wisdom to control Scripture, where will it end? Soon one person will reject the doctrine of the devil as opposed to his reason; another will dismiss that of eternal punishment as wounding his heart; a third will hide the doctrine of atonement under commentaries that suffocate it. There will no longer be a definitive faith, because there will no longer be divine authority. Scripture cannot be controlled except by Scripture, and one *it is written* can only be solidly opposed by an *again it is written*.

ON SANCTIFICATION

Satan sees a Christian who is applying himself diligently to his salvation, praying without ceasing, meditating on the Scriptures day and night, and being careful to avoid the defilement of the world. He has sought in vain to divert him from prayer, to make him doubt God's Word, and to inspire in him the love of the present age. Then Satan takes his Bible in hand (you just saw that he has one), and begins to preach to him. "Say, my friend, what is this load with which you are burdening yourself? Do you have to get all out of breath to serve God? To look at you, one would have good reason to loath godliness. I will show you an easier and more orthodox way, for in the end your sanctification is God's work, not yours. Let loose a little; follow the leading of your heart, and let God act. It is written, 'For it is God who works in you, both to will and to work for his good pleasure'" (Philippians 2:13).[21]

Yes, follow the leading of your heart, and the devil will be more tranquil on your account, I can easily believe that. Ah, my brother, reply to this "holy Satan," as Luther somewhere calls him, "Again it is written, 'Work out your own salvation with fear and trembling' (Philippians 2:12) and 'Strive to enter through the narrow door'" (Luke 13:24).

ON PREACHING

Satan wants to take a minister of the gospel whose powerful preaching batters down "the gates of hell" (Matthew 16:18) and bring him to a state of laxness. He has sought in vain to stop him in his holy work through discouragement, through vain glory, and through the world's hostility. Now he has recourse to Scripture and says to him, "Man of God, why

---

[21] See also Romans 9:16. [A.M.]

do you take such great pains over the spiritual nurture you owe your people? Can't you say things that are holy, true, and healthy without growing pale that way over your Bible and your books? Do things more simply. Trust in your God-given ability to speak; yield to the Holy Spirit, and say what he puts in your heart. Thus you will bring more honor to the Lord, not to mention the time you will gain for his service. It is written, 'What you are to say will be given to you in that hour. For it is not you who speak, but the Spirit of your Father speaking through you' " (Matthew 10:19-20).

There, my friends, is a lovely trap set out for your natural laziness. If you fall into it, you have reason to fear that your preaching will become lifeless, as lifeless as that of so many other servants of God who, beneath lovely pretexts, avoid difficult labor (see 2 Samuel 24:24) in order to give themselves over to effortless improvisation. But here is your deliverance. Reply, "Again it is written, 'Devote yourself to the public reading of Scripture, to exhortation, to teaching. Do not neglect the gift you have. . . . Keep a close watch on yourself and on the teaching. Persist in this, for by so doing you will save both yourself and your hearers' " (1 Timothy 4:13,14,16).[22]

THE BIBLE'S BALANCE

The same principle applies to Satan's other scriptural temptations. Stay on your guard against the devil's exegesis, and fight it quite simply with Scripture itself. What it omits in one place, it will tell you in another. It is as if the Bible judges as worthy to penetrate the depths of its thought only those who take the trouble to compare and harmonize its varied teachings.

---

[22] See also Romans 12:6-8. [A.M.]

If it is written, "One is justified by faith apart from works of the law" (Romans 3:28), it is also written, "Faith apart from works is dead" (James 2:26).

If it is written, "Neither be called instructors, for you have one instructor, the Christ" (Matthew 23:10), it is also written, "Obey your leaders and submit to them, for they are keeping watch over your souls" (Hebrews 13:17).

If it is written, "Your Father knows what you need before you ask him" (Matthew 6:8), it is also written, "Ask, and it will be given to you; seek, and you will find; knock, and it will be opened to you" (Matthew 7:7; Luke 11:9).

If it is written, "I am sure that neither death nor life, nor angels nor rulers, nor things present nor things to come, . . . nor anything else in all creation, will be able to separate us from the love of God in Christ Jesus" (Romans 8:38-39), it is also written, "Blessed is the one who fears the LORD always" (Proverbs 28:14).

If it is written, "To the pure, all things are pure" (Titus 1:15), it is also written, "Abstain from every form of evil" (1 Thessalonians 5:22).

POSSESSING THE SCRIPTURES

My dear brothers, you just learned from Jesus' example in responding to the tempter's threefold attack how to use the Scriptures in combating temptation. But to follow that example, you need to know the Scriptures as Jesus did.

Don't be astonished that I talk about Jesus' knowledge of the Scriptures, for we cannot repeat often enough that, though Jesus was the Son of God, he was also the Son of man, and it is as the Son of man that he was victorious in the wilderness. How familiar with the Scriptures one must be to quote them so appropriately and adapt them so exactly to the infinite variety of human temptations! Jesus moves and finds his way through the Scriptures with as much ease as we move and find our way through a city that we have traversed again and again in every direction since childhood and whose every street, every square, every house is engraved in our memory.

A COMPREHENSIVE KNOWLEDGE

That is how you need to possess the Scriptures. It is not through vague approximations that you can hope to battle the enemy effectively. The more precise you are in your use of Scripture, the stronger you will be. How do you know? There might be some special declaration of the Holy Spirit pertaining to the special temptation that weighs on you, a temptation to which no other declaration could fully respond. You need to discover it. Scripture must be for you like an arsenal so well studied that you can immediately place your hand on the weapon required for your defense. It must be like a pharmacy in such good order that you can instantly find the remedy needed for your healing.

You cannot always have your Bible in front of you, so if you want never to be without it, you need to carry it in your heart. Yet to do so, what study of the Scriptures, what constant reading, what depth of meditation is required!

Very well! All of that is nothing more than what God himself laid out for us. "Blessed is the man" whose "delight is in the law of the LORD, and on his law he meditates day and night" (Psalm 1:1-2). "This book of the law shall not depart from your mouth, but you shall meditate on it day and night" (Joshua 1:8).

All of that is nothing more than what was done by the holy men who are offered for our emulation. "Oh how I love your law! It is my meditation all the day. . . . My eyes are awake before the watches of the night, that I may meditate on your promise. . . . At midnight I rise to praise you, because of your righteous rules" (Psalm 119:97,148,62).

All of that is nothing more than what was given to us in the example of our own fathers, even in their times of wilderness or martyrdom. One could say of these old witnesses that if the Bible were lost, the combined memories of several of them would suffice to rewrite it in its entirety.[23]

What then, oh my God, is the state into which we have fallen? What ignorance of the Scriptures amongst our people! What ignorance of the Scriptures amongst our pastors! Lord, give us back the former days!

A THOROUGH UNDERSTANDING

But this knowledge of the Scriptures through which one keeps them in his memory, even if it extended to knowing them by heart from one end to the other, is still not what is most important in imitating Jesus. What enables Jesus to be victorious through the Scriptures is not that he knows the words; it is that he grasps their meaning and their spirit. The Bible contains maxims of the Kingdom of heaven, but they are clothed in an earthly form, so that only someone who knows how to separate the divine thoughts from their human envelope can really understand it. That is what Jesus does in my text. He does not limit himself to the book's surface; he sounds "the thoughts and intentions" (Hebrews 4:12) of that which "is written."

To prove this I need only the first of his three quotations: "Man shall not live by bread alone, but by every word that comes from the mouth of God." Let us agree that if you were tempted as the Lord was, you would never have dreamt of defending yourself with that verse, and it might often have passed beneath your gaze without you seeing what Jesus found there. You would have seen the marvelous fact of

---

[23] This refers to the difficult days during which the Protestants in France were severely persecuted.

manna granted to the Israelites in place of bread.[24] You
would have seen a pledge of hope for a people placed in a
situation analogous to theirs, if that situation could ever be
repeated. Finally you would have seen an encouraging testimony to God's love for his creatures and of his faithfulness
to his people. But there is where your exegesis would end,
bound to history and the miracle.

How much more penetrating is Jesus' exegesis! He digs
down to the deepest levels, clarifying even the intimate
thoughts of the Holy Spirit. Beneath the history, beneath the
miracle, beneath all that takes place, he discovers a per-
manent general principle: *All power resides in God's Word,
which is not limited to the specific means it usually employs.*
It is at this depth that Israel's temptation and Jesus' meet—so
to speak—underground and at their root, so that Moses'
words interpreted by Jesus Christ apply just as well to the
latter as to the former. More than that, they apply equally to
the temptations of God's children in every age. And yet, note
it well, this broad and varied application of Moses' words has
nothing forced or arbitrary about it. There is neither allegory
nor double meaning here—nothing but the deep thought of
the Holy Spirit found in the deep language of Scripture, the
true substance in the true form.

There, my dear friends, is Jesus' exegesis, a spiritual, sub-
stantive exegesis that is equally accessible to the scholar and
the simple. It is as attractive to the spirit as it is nourishing to
the soul. Beside it, our ordinary exegesis is superficial and
cold, even when it is most scholarly and conscientious. That
is because ours is encumbered by the things of earth, while
Jesus' is lifted up to the thoughts of heaven. What a lovely

---

[24] The full text of the verse reads, "And he humbled you and let you
hunger and fed you with manna, which you did not know, nor did your
fathers know, that he might make you know that man does not live by
bread alone, but man lives by every word that comes from the mouth of
the LORD."

book the Bible would become—and, alas, what a new book—if it were studied in this spirit! The Bible, if I may say so, is heaven spoken, but we must extricate that heaven from the words that conceal it even as they reveal it. That is what Jesus is teaching us.

PRAYERFUL SEEKING

Moreover, no commentary can provide this exegesis for us. We must seek it on our knees, saying to God, "Open my eyes, that I may behold wondrous things out of your law" (Psalm 119:18). That is when one receives "the testimony of God . . . in himself" (1 John 5:9-10). That is when what is written on the heart corresponds so exactly to what is written in the book that the same spirit must be recognized in both. We just said that the Bible is heaven spoken; the Bible listened to in this way would be heaven seen, felt, and lived!

CONCLUSION

Here we are, my dear brothers, at the end of the course we set out on. For three Sundays I have engaged you with Jesus' temptations in the wilderness. That is not too much time for such a vast and instructive subject. As for me, I will recall with special emotion these three weeks during which I have constantly reflected on the battle that my Savior underwent, on the victory that he gained, and on the weapon that made him victorious. I have found something particularly meaningful and healthy in that reflection, and I hope that by God's faithfulness it will not have been without blessing for me and for you.

FOR ALL BELIEVERS

Carry yourself often back into the wilderness. Whenever the number and magnitude of your temptations nearly overwhelms you, remember Jesus tempted as you are in all things. Whenever you are in doubt about the possibility of resisting, remember Jesus crushing Satan under his feet and promising to crush him under your feet as well. Finally, whenever you are uncertain of the means needed to be victorious, remember Jesus deflecting all the adversary's blows, finally forcing him to turn his back, using only the Sword of the Holy Spirit.

FOR FUTURE MINISTERS

And you, my future yokefellows, I do not want to leave this subject without addressing to you a special exhortation, which I commend for your most serious attention. Jesus' temptation is found placed between the end of his personal preparation and the beginning of his public life. There is an analogous moment for you. It is the interval that separates the end of your studies from the beginning of your ministry. Take care of that interval; it can shape your entire career. Consecrate it to a spiritual retreat. Spend it with Jesus struggling in his solitude, and when you enter the ministry, may one recognize in you a man coming out of the wilderness.

From the wilderness, and not from the world. If you are filled with memories of the world, if you have been breathing the impure atmosphere of its vanities and pleasures, you are not fit for the service of Jesus Christ.

From the wilderness, and not from Nazareth. If you are ruled by your family affections, if in choosing a position, you place first emphasis on a father or a mother, on a wife or a child, you are not fit for the service of Jesus Christ.

From the wilderness, and not from the school. If you are still covered with the dust of the academy, if your faith and your knowledge are only those of books, you are not fit for the service of Jesus Christ.

Jesus Christ needs servants who are detached from the world, free from obligations toward their fellow creatures, nourished under the teaching of the Holy Spirit. Either be men of the wilderness or do not be men of the Church! Amen.

OTHER TITLES FROM SOLID GROUND

In addition to Monod's *Jesus Tempted in the Wilderness,* Solid Ground Christian Books has reprinted several volumes from the Puritan era, such as the following:

The Complete Works of Thomas Manton (in 22 volumes)
A Body of Divinity by Archbishop James Ussher
An Exposition of Hebrews by William Gouge
A Short Explanation of Hebrews by David Dickson
An Exposition of the Epistle of Jude by Thomas Jenkyn
A Commentary on the New Testament by John Trapp
Gospel Sonnets by Ralph Erskine
Heaven Upon Earth by James Janeway
The Marrow of True Justification by Benjamin Keach
The Travels of True Godliness by Benjamin Keach
The Redeemer's Tears Wept Over Lost Souls by John Howe
Commentary on the Second Epistle of Peter by Thomas Adams
The Christian Warfare by John Downame
An Exposition of the Ten Commandments by Ezekiel Hopkins
The Harmony of the Divine Attributes by William Bates
The Communicant's Companion by Matthew Henry
The Secret of Communion with God by Matthew Henry

View at www.solid-ground-books.com

Call us at 205-443-0311

LaVergne, TN USA
14 September 2010
196981LV00002B/1/P

9 781599 252469